Practice Planners™

Arthur E. Jongsma, Jr.. Series Editor

W9-BRM-637

Helping therapists help their clients...

Over 150,000 Practice *Planners*™ sold...

 WILEY

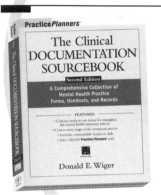

The
Complete Adult
Psychotherapy
Treatment Planner

PRACTICE *PLANNERS*™ SERIES

Treatment *Planners*

The Complete Adult Psychotherapy Treatment Planner, Second Edition •
0471-31924-4 *book only* • 0471-31957-0 *book + disk*

The Child and Adolescent Psychotherapy Treatment Planner •
0471-15647-7

The Chemical Dependence Treatment Planner • 0471-23795-7 *book only*
• 0471-23794-9 *book + disk*

The Continuum of Care Treatment Planner • 0471-19568-5 *book only*
• 0471-19569-3 *book + disk*

The Couples Psychotherapy Treatment Planner • 0471-24711-1 *book only*
• 0471-24710-3 *book + disk*

The Employee Assistance Treatment Planner • 0471-24709-X *book only*
• 0471-24730-8 *book + disk*

The Pastoral Counseling Treatment Planner • 0471-25416-9 *book only*
• 0471-25417-7 *book + disk*

The Older Adult Psychotherapy Treatment Planner • 0471-29574-4
book only • 0471-29581-7 *book + disk*

The Behavioral Medicine Treatment Planner • 0471-31923-6 *book only*
• 0471-31926-0 *book + disk*

Homework *Planners*

Brief Therapy Homework Planner • 0471-24611-5
Brief Couples Therapy Homework Planner • 0471-29511-6
The Chemical Dependence Homework Planner • 0471-32452-3
The Brief Child Therapy Homework Planner • 0471-32366-7
The Brief Adolescent Therapy Homework Planner • 0471-34465-6

Documentation *Sourcebooks*

The Clinical Documentation Sourcebook • 0471-17934-5
The Forensic Documentation Sourcebook • 0471-25459-2
The Psychotherapy Documentation Primer • 0471-28990-6
The Chemical Dependence Treatment Documentation Sourcebook •
0471-31285-1
The Child Clinical Documentation Sourcebook • 0471-29111-0
The Couples and Family Clinical Documentation Sourcebook •
0471-25234-4
The Clinical Documentation Sourcebook, Second Edition •
0471-32692-5

The ERICHA SCOTT Complete Adult Psychotherapy Treatment Planner

SECOND EDITION

Arthur E. Jongsma, Jr.

L. Mark Peterson

JOHN WILEY & SONS, INC.

New York • Chichester • Weinheim • Brisbane • Singapore • Toronto

Copyright © 1999 by Arthur E. Jongsma, Jr., and L. Mark Peterson.
All rights reserved.
Published by John Wiley & Sons, Inc.
Published simultaneously in Canada.

All references to diagnostic codes and the entire content of Appendix B are reprinted with permission from the *Diagnostic and Statistical Manual of Mental Disorders, Fourth Edition.* Copyright 1994. American Psychiatric Association.

Designations used by companies to distinguish their products are often claimed as trademarks. In all instances where John Wiley & Sons, Inc. is aware of a claim, the product names appear in initial capital or all capital letters. Readers, however, should contact the appropriate companies for more complete information regarding trademarks and registration.

This publication is designed to provide accurate and authoritative information in regard to the subject matter covered. It is sold with the understanding that the publisher is not engaged in rendering professional services. If legal, accounting, medical, psychological or any other expert assistance is required, the services of a competent professional person should be sought.

Library of Congress Cataloging-in-Publication Data:
Jongsma, Arthur E., 1943-
    The complete adult psychotherapy treatment planner / Arthur E.
Jongsma, Jr., and L. Mark Peterson. — 2nd ed.
        p.   cm. — (Practice planner series)
    Rev. ed. of: The complete psychotherapy treatment planner. c1995.
    Includes bibliographical references.
    ISBN 0-471-31924-4 (pbk. : alk. paper). — ISBN 0-471-31957-0 (pbk./disk:
alk. paper)
    1. Mental illness—Treatment—Planning—Handbooks, manuals, etc.
2. Psychiatric records—Handbooks, manuals, etc.   I. Peterson, L.
Mark.   II. Jongsma, Arthur E., 1943-   Complete psychotherapy
treatment planner.   III. Title.   IV. Series: Practice planners.
    [DNLM: 1. Psychotherapy handbooks.   2. Patient Care Planning
handbooks. WM 34J79c 1999]
RC480.5.J664   1999
616.89′14′068—dc21
DNLM/DLC
for Library of Congress   98-39258
                                                                          CIP

Printed in the United States of America.

10 9 8 7 6 5 4 3

We dedicate this book to our most influential
teachers and mentors early in our professional journey:

Dr. Solomon E. Feldman
Dr. Richard A. Westmaas
Dr. Richard Brown
Dr. Jack Carr

CONTENTS

PREFACE

This second edition of *The Complete Adult Psychotherapy Treatment Planner* was mandated by the overwhelming success of the first edition published in 1995 as the original book in Wiley's Practice Planner series. Since that original book was published, we have developed a number of specialized practice planners. These specialized planners are available in electronic version on floppy disk which allows the information to be imported into *TheraScribe 3.0: The Computerized Assistant to Psychotherapy Treatment Planning.* The Practice Planner series also includes several Psychotherapy Homework Planners that are coordinated with the Treatment Planners, or which can be used independently. Several Documentation Sourcebooks, containing useful examples of clinical record keeping forms and handouts round out the Practice Planner series.

The second edition is thoroughly revised from its predecessor, *The Complete Psychotherapy Treatment Planner.* First, the Objectives and Interventions of every chapter have been reorganized to improve their logical flow as part of the treatment process. Second, each chapter has been expanded by the addition of dozens of new Objectives and Interventions. Third, the wording of some Objectives and Interventions has been made more precise. Fourth, minor revisions have been made to a few Definition and Goal statements. Finally, in response to reader feedback, five totally new chapters covering Attention Deficit Disorder—Adult, Borderline Personality, Chronic Pain, Financial Stress, and Posttraumatic Stress Disorder—have been added to the book. We hope these changes to the original content and the addition of new Objectives and Intervention as well as new chapters continue to meet the need for fresh ideas and concise but precise wording for treatment plans.

As with the other Planners, this book would not have been possible without the forbearance of our families. We are especially grateful to our wives, Judy Jongsma and Cherry Peterson, for their encouragement and support during the months of manuscript preparation. Jen

Byrne deserves our appreciation for her patient hours of labor with the word processor, always wanting to get everything just right. Finally, Kelly Franklin, our editor at Wiley, continues to be the foresighted energetic force behind the Practice Planner series. Thank you, Kelly.

Arthur E. Jongsma, Jr.
L. Mark Peterson

INTRODUCTION

Since the early 1960s, formalized treatment planning has gradually become a vital aspect of the entire health-care delivery system, whether it is treatment related to physical health, mental health, child welfare, or substance abuse. What started in the medical sector in the 1960s spread into the mental health sector in the 1970s as clinics, psychiatric hospitals, agencies, and so on, began to seek accreditation from bodies such as the Joint Commission on Accreditation of Healthcare Organizations (JCAHO) to qualify for third-party reimbursements. For most treatment providers to achieve accreditation, they had to begin developing and strengthening their documentation skills in the area of treatment planning. Previously, most mental health and substance abuse treatment providers had, at best, a "bare-bones" plan that looked similar for most of the individuals they treated. As a result, clients were uncertain as to what they were trying to attain in mental health treatment. Goals were vague, objectives were nonexistent, and interventions were applied equally to all clients. Outcome data were not measurable, and neither the treatment provider nor the client knew exactly when treatment was complete. The initial development of rudimentary treatment plans made inroads toward addressing some of these issues.

With the advent of managed care in the 1980s, treatment planning has taken on even more importance. Managed care systems *insist* that clinicians move rapidly from assessment of the problem to the formulation and implementation of the treatment plan. The goal of most managed care companies is to expedite the treatment process by prompting the client and treatment provider to focus on identifying and changing behavioral problems as quickly as possible. Treatment plans must be specific as to the problems and interventions, individualized to meet the client's needs and goals, and measurable in terms of setting milestones that can be used to chart the patient's progress. Pressure from third-party payers, accrediting agencies, and other outside parties has therefore increased the need for clinicians to produce effective, high-quality treatment plans in a short time frame. However, many mental health providers have little experience in treatment plan development. Our purpose in writing this book is to clarify, simplify, and accelerate the treatment planning process.

TREATMENT PLAN UTILITY

Detailed written treatment plans can benefit not only the client, therapist, treatment team, insurance community, and treatment agency, but also the overall psychotherapy profession. The client is served by a written plan because it stipulates the issues that are the focus of the treatment process. It is very easy for both provider and client to lose sight of what the issues were that brought the patient into therapy. The treatment plan is a guide that structures the focus of the therapeutic contract. Since issues can change as therapy progresses, the treatment plan must be viewed as a dynamic document that can and must be updated to reflect any major change of problem, definition, goal, objective, or intervention.

Clients and therapists benefit from the treatment plan, which forces both to think about therapy outcomes. Behaviorally stated, measurable objectives clearly focus the treatment endeavor. Clients no longer have to wonder what therapy is trying to accomplish. Clear objectives also allow the patient to channel effort into specific changes that will lead to the long-term goal of problem resolution. Therapy is no longer a vague contract to just talk honestly and openly about emotions and cognitions until the client feels better. Both client and therapist are concentrating on specifically stated objectives using specific interventions.

Providers are aided by treatment plans because they are forced to think analytically and critically about therapeutic interventions that are best suited for objective attainment for the patient. Therapists were traditionally trained to "follow the patient," but now a formalized plan is the guide to the treatment process. The therapist must give advance attention to the technique, approach, assignment, or cathartic target that will form the basis for interventions.

Clinicians benefit from clear documentation of treatment because it provides a measure of added protection from possible patient litigation. Malpractice suits are increasing in frequency and insurance premiums are soaring. The first line of defense against allegations is a complete clinical record detailing the treatment process. A written, individualized, formal treatment plan that is the guideline for the therapeutic process, that has been reviewed and signed by the client, and that is coupled with problem-oriented progress notes is a powerful defense against exaggerated or false claims.

A well-crafted treatment plan that clearly stipulates presenting problems and intervention strategies facilitates the treatment process carried out by team members in inpatient, residential, or intensive outpatient settings. Good communication between team members about what approach is being implemented and who is responsible for which intervention is critical. Team meetings to discuss patient treatment used to be the only source of interaction between providers; often, therapeutic conclusions or assignments were not recorded. Now, a thorough treatment plan stipulates in writing the details of objectives and the varied interventions (pharmacologic, milieu, group therapy, didactic, recreational, individual therapy, etc.) and who will implement them.

Every treatment agency or institution is constantly looking for ways to increase the quality and uniformity of the documentation in the clinical record. A standardized, written treatment plan with problem definitions, goals, objectives, and interventions in every client's file enhances that uniformity of documentation. This uniformity eases the task of record reviewers inside and outside the agency. Outside reviewers, such as JCAHO, insist on documentation that clearly outlines assessment, treatment, progress, and discharge status.

The demand for accountability from third-party payers and health maintenance organizations (HMOs) is partially satisfied by a written treatment plan and complete progress notes. More and more managed care systems are demanding a structured therapeutic contract that has measurable objectives and explicit interventions. Clinicians cannot avoid this move toward being accountable to those outside the treatment process.

The psychotherapy profession stands to benefit from the use of more precise, measurable objectives to evaluate success in mental health treatment. With the advent of detailed treatment plans, outcome data can be more easily collected for interventions that are effective in achieving specific goals.

HOW TO DEVELOP A TREATMENT PLAN

The process of developing a treatment plan involves a logical series of steps that build on each other much like constructing a house. The foundation of any effective treatment plan is the data gathered in a thorough biopsychosocial assessment. As the client presents himself or herself for treatment, the clinician must sensitively listen to and understand what the client struggles with in terms of family of origin issues, current stressors, emotional status, social network, physical health, coping skills, interpersonal conflicts, self-esteem, and so on. Assessment data may be gathered from a social history, physical exam, clinical interview, psychological testing, or contact with a client's significant others. The integration of the data by the clinician or the multidisciplinary treatment team members is critical for understanding the client, as is an awareness of the basis of the client's struggle. We have identified six specific steps for developing an effective treatment plan based on the assessment data.

Step One: Problem Selection

Although the client may discuss a variety of issues during the assessment, the clinician must ferret out the most significant problems on which to focus the treatment process. Usually a *primary* problem will surface, and *secondary* problems may also be evident. Some *other* problems may have to be set aside as not urgent enough to require treatment at this time. An effective treatment plan can only deal with a few selected problems or treatment will lose its direction. This *Planner* offers 39 problems from which to select those that most accurately represent your client's presenting issues.

As the problems to be selected become clear to the clinician or the treatment team, it is important to include opinions from the client as to his or her prioritization of issues for which help is being sought. A client's motivation to participate in and cooperate with the treatment process depends, to some extent, on the degree to which treatment addresses his or her greatest needs.

Step Two: Problem Definition

Each individual client presents with unique nuances as to how a problem behaviorally reveals itself in his or her life. Therefore, each problem that is selected for treatment focus requires a specific definition about how it is evidenced in the particular client. The symptom pattern should be associated with diagnostic criteria and codes such as those found in the *Diagnostic and Statistical Manual* or the *International Classification of Diseases*. The *Planner,* following the pattern established by *DSM-IV,* offers such behaviorally specific definition statements to choose from or to serve as a model for your own personally crafted statements. You will find several behavior symptoms or syndromes listed that may characterize one of the 39 presenting problems.

Step Three: Goal Development

The next step in treatment plan development is that of setting broad goals for the resolution of the target problem. These statements need not be crafted in measurable terms but can be global, long-term goals that indicate a desired positive outcome to the treatment procedures. The *Planner* suggests several possible goal statements for each problem, but one statement is all that is required in a treatment plan.

Step Four: Objective Construction

In contrast to long-term goals, objectives must be stated in behaviorally measurable language. It must be clear when the client has achieved the established objectives; therefore, vague, subjective objectives are not acceptable. Review agencies (e.g., JCAHO), HMOs, and managed care organizations insist that psychological treatment outcome be measurable. The objectives presented in this *Planner* are designed to meet this demand for accountability. Numerous alternatives are presented to allow construction of a variety of treatment plan possibilities for the same presenting problem. The clinician must exercise professional judgment as to which objectives are most appropriate for a given client.

Each objective should be developed as a step toward attaining the broad treatment goal. In essence, objectives can be thought of as a series of steps that, when completed, will result in the achievement of the long-term goal. There should be at least two objectives for each problem, but the clinician may construct as many as are necessary for goal achievement. Target attainment dates should be listed for each objective. New objectives should be added to the plan as the individual's treatment progresses. When all the necessary objectives have been achieved, the client should have resolved the target problem successfully.

Step Five: Intervention Creation

Interventions are the actions of the clinician designed to help the client complete the objectives. There should be at least one intervention for every objective. If the client does not accomplish the objective after the initial intervention, new interventions should be added to the plan.

Interventions should be selected on the basis of the client's needs and the treatment provider's full therapeutic repertoire. This *Planner* contains interventions from a broad range of therapeutic approaches, including cognitive, dynamic, behavioral, pharmacologic, family-oriented, and solution-focused brief therapy. Other interventions may be written by the provider to reflect his or her own training and experience. The addition of new problems, definitions, goals, objectives, and interventions to those found in the *Planner* is encouraged because doing so adds to the database for future reference and use.

Some suggested interventions listed in the *Planner* refer to specific books that can be assigned to the client for adjunctive bibliotherapy. Appendix A contains a full bibliographic reference list of these materials. The books are arranged under each problem for which they are appropriate as assigned reading for clients. When a book is used as part of an intervention plan, it should be reviewed with the client after it is read, enhancing the application of the content of the book to the specific client's circumstances. For further information about self-help books, mental health professionals may wish to consult *The Authoritative Guide to Self-Help Books* (1994) by Santrock, Minnett, and Campbell (available from The Guilford Press, New York, NY).

Assigning an intervention to a specific provider is most relevant if the patient is being treated by a team in an inpatient, residential, or intensive outpatient setting. Within these settings, personnel other than the primary clinician may be responsible for implementing a specific intervention. Review agencies require that the responsible provider's name be stipulated for every intervention.

Step Six: Diagnosis Determination

The determination of an appropriate diagnosis is based on an evaluation of the client's complete clinical presentation. The clinician must compare the behavioral, cognitive, emotional, and interpersonal symptoms that the client presents to the criteria for diagnosis of a mental illness condition as described in *DSM-IV*. The issue of differential diagnosis is admittedly a difficult one that research has shown to have rather low interrater reliability. Psychologists have also been trained to think more in terms of maladaptive behavior than disease labels. In spite of these factors, diagnosis is a reality that exists in the world of mental health care and it is a necessity for third-party reimbursement. (However, recently, managed care agencies are more interested in behavioral indices that are exhibited by the client than the actual diagnosis.) It is the clinician's thorough knowledge of *DSM-IV* criteria and a complete understanding of the client assessment data that contribute to the most reliable, valid diagnosis. An accurate assessment of behavioral indicators will also contribute to more effective treatment planning.

HOW TO USE THIS PLANNER

Our experience has taught us that learning the skills of effective treatment plan writing can be a tedious and difficult process for many clinicians. It is more stressful to try to develop this expertise when under the pressure of increased patient load and short time frames placed on clinicians today by managed care systems. The documentation demands can be overwhelming when we must move quickly from assessment to treatment plan to progress notes. In the process, we must be very specific about how and when objectives can be achieved, and how progress is exhibited in each client. *The Complete Adult Psychotherapy Treatment Planner* was developed as a tool to aid clinicians in writing a treatment plan in a rapid manner that is clear, specific, and highly individualized according to the following progression:

1. Choose one presenting problem (Step One) you have identified through your assessment process. Locate the corresponding page number for that problem in the *Planner*'s table of contents.
2. Select two or three of the listed behavioral definitions (Step Two) and record them in the appropriate section on your treatment plan form. Feel free to add your own defining statement if you determine that your client's behavioral manifestation of the identified problem is not listed. (Note that while our design for treatment planning is vertical, it will work equally well on plan forms formatted horizontally.)
3. Select a single long-term goal (Step Three) and again write the selection, exactly as it is written in the *Planner* or in some appropriately modified form, in the corresponding area of your own form.
4. Review the listed objectives for this problem and select the ones that you judge to be clinically indicated for your client (Step Four). Remember, it is recommended that you select at least two objectives for each problem. Add a target date or the number of sessions allocated for the attainment of each objective.
5. Choose relevant interventions (Step Five). The *Planner* offers suggested interventions related to each objective in the parentheses following the objective statement. But do not limit yourself to those interventions. The entire list is eclectic and may offer options that are more tailored to your theoretical approach or preferred way of working with clients. Also, just as with definitions, goals, and objectives, there is space allowed for you to enter your own interventions into the *Planner*. This allows you to refer to these entries when you create a plan around this problem in the future. You will have to assign responsibility to a spe-

cific person for implementation of each intervention if the treatment is being carried out by a multidisciplinary team.

6. Several *DSM-IV* diagnoses are listed at the end of each chapter that are commonly associated with a client who has this problem. These diagnoses are meant to be suggestions for clinical consideration. Select a diagnosis listed or assign a more appropriate choice from the *DSM-IV* (Step Six).

Note: To accommodate those practitioners who tend to plan treatment in terms of diagnostic labels rather than presenting problems, Appendix B lists all of the *DSM-IV* diagnoses that have been presented in the various presenting problem chapters as suggestions for consideration. Each diagnosis is followed by the presenting problem that has been associated with that diagnosis. Providers may look up the presenting problems for a selected diagnosis to review definitions, goals, objectives, and interventions that may be appropriate for their clients with that diagnosis.

Congratulations! You should now have a complete, individualized treatment plan that is ready for immediate implementation and presentation to the client. It should resemble the format of the sample plan presented on the facing page.

A FINAL NOTE

One important aspect of effective treatment planning is that each plan should be tailored to the individual client's problems and needs. Treatment plans should not be mass produced, even if clients have similar problems. The individual's strengths and weaknesses, unique stressors, social network, family circumstances, and symptom patterns *must* be considered in developing a treatment strategy. Drawing upon our own years of clinical experience, we have put together a variety of treatment choices. These statements can be combined in thousands of permutations to develop detailed treatment plans. Relying on their own good judgment, clinicians can easily select the statements that are appropriate for the individuals they are treating. In addition, we encourage readers to add their own definitions, goals, objectives, and interventions to the existing samples. It is our hope that *The Complete Adult Psychotherapy Treatment Planner* will promote effective, creative treatment planning—a process that will ultimately benefit the client, the clinician, and the mental health community.

SAMPLE TREATMENT PLAN

Problem: ANGER MANAGEMENT

Definition: Overreaction of hostility to insignificant irritants.

Use of verbally abusive language.

History of explosive aggressive outbursts out of proportion to any precipitating stressors leading to assaultive acts or destruction of property.

Goals: Develop an awareness of current angry behaviors, clarifying origins of and alternatives to aggressive anger.

Objectives	Interventions
1. Verbalize an increased awareness of anger expression patterns (4/20/99).	1. Confront/reflect angry behaviors in group and individual sessions.
	2. Assign patient to read the book *Of Course You're Angry* (Rosellini and Worden) or *The Angry Book* (Rubin).
2. Identify pain and hurt of past or current life that fuels anger (5/29/99).	1. Assign patient to list experiences of life that have hurt and led to anger.
3. Verbalize feelings of anger in a controlled, assertive way (6/20/99).	1. Assign assertiveness-training classes.
	2. Using role-playing techniques, assist patient in developing non-self-defeating ways (e.g., assertive use of "I messages") of handling angry feelings.

Diagnosis: 312.34   Intermittent Explosive Disorder

ANGER MANAGEMENT

BEHAVIORAL DEFINITIONS

1. History of explosive aggressive outbursts out of proportion to any precipitating stressors leading to assaultive acts or destruction of property.
2. Overreaction of hostility to insignificant irritants.
3. Swift and harsh judgement statements made to or about others.
4. Body language of tense muscles (e.g., clenched fist or jaw, glaring looks, or refusal to make eye contact).
5. Use of passive-aggressive patterns (social withdrawal due to anger, lack of complete or timely compliance in following directions or rules, complaining about authority figures behind their backs, or nonparticipation in meeting expected behavioral norms).
6. Consistent pattern of challenging or disrespectful treatment of authority figures.
7. Use of verbally abusive language.

—. _____
   _____
   _____
—. _____
   _____
   _____
—. _____
   _____

LONG-TERM GOALS

1. Decrease overall intensity and frequency of angry feelings and increase ability to recognize and appropriately express angry feelings as they occur.

2. Develop an awareness of current angry behaviors, clarifying origins of and alternatives to aggressive anger.
3. Come to an awareness and acceptance of angry feelings while developing better control and more serenity.
4. Become capable of handling angry feelings in constructive ways that enhance daily functioning.

—. _____
_____
—. _____
_____
—. _____
_____

SHORT-TERM OBJECTIVES

1. Verbally acknowledge that he/she is angry. (1, 2)
2. Identify targets of and causes for anger. (2, 3, 4)
3. Verbalize increased awareness of anger expression patterns. (2, 5, 6)
4. Verbalize how influential people in growing up have modeled anger expressions. (2, 7)
5. Identify pain and hurt of past or current life that fuels anger. (2, 8, 9)
6. Verbalize feelings of anger in a controlled, assertive way. (10, 11, 12, 17)
7. Decrease the number and duration of angry outbursts. (10, 13)
8. Utilize relaxation techniques to cope with angry feelings. (14)

THERAPEUTIC INTERVENTIONS

1. Assist patient in coming to the realization that he/she is angry.
2. Assign patient to read the book *Of Course You're Angry* (Rosellini and Worden) or *The Angry Book* (Rubin).
3. Ask patient to keep a daily journal in which he/she documents persons, situations, and so on that cause anger, irritation, or disappointment.
4. Assign and process a thorough list of all targets of and causes for anger.
5. Confront/reflect angry behaviors that occur within sessions.
6. Refer patient to an anger management class or group.
7. Assist patient in identifying ways key life figures, such

9. Verbalize increased awareness of how past ways of handling angry feelings have had a negative impact. (13, 15, 16)

10. Decrease verbal and physical manifestations of anger, aggression, or violence while increasing awareness and acceptance of feelings. (12, 17)

11. Verbalize increased awareness of and ability to react to hot buttons or anger triggers in a nonaggressive manner. (10, 18, 19)

12. Write an angry letter to target of anger and process this letter with therapist. (20, 21)

13. Verbalize recognition of how holding on to angry feelings freezes you and hands control over to others and cite the advantages of forgiveness. (22, 23)

14. Write a letter of forgiveness to perpetrator of past or present pain and process this letter with therapist. (24)

__. _____

_____

__. _____

_____

__. _____

_____

as father, mother, and teachers, have expressed angry feelings and how positively or negatively these experiences have influenced the way patient handles anger.

8. Assign patient to list the experiences of life that have hurt and led to anger.

9. Empathize and clarify feelings of hurt and anger tied to traumas of past.

10. Assign assertiveness training classes.

11. Process patient's angry feelings or angry outbursts that have recently occurred and review alternative behaviors available.

12. Using role-playing techniques, assist patient in developing non-self-defeating ways (e.g., assertive use of "I messages") of handling angry feelings.

13. Assign a specific exercise from the *Anger Work Out Book* (Weisinger) or similar workbook and process exercise with patient.

14. Teach patient relaxation techniques (e.g., deep breathing, positive imagery, deep muscle relaxation, etc.) to cope with initial response to angry feelings when they occur.

15. Ask patient to list ways anger has negatively impacted him/her in daily life. Process list with patient.

16. Expand patient's awareness of the negative affects that anger has on his/her body.

17. Use empty chair technique to coach patient in expressing angry feelings in a constructive, non-self-defeating manner.

18. Assist patient in developing the ability to recognize his/her hot buttons/triggers that lead to angry explosions.

19. Train patient in Rational Emotive Therapy (RET) techniques for coping with feelings of anger, frustration, and rage.

20. Ask patient to write an angry letter to parents, spouse, or whomever, focusing on the reasons for his/her anger toward that person. Process letter in session.

21. Encourage patient to express and release while in session feelings of anger or rage, and violent fantasies or plots for revenge.

22. Discuss forgiveness of perpetrators of pain as a process of letting go of anger.

23. Assign patient to read the book *Forgive and Forget* (Smedes).

24. Ask patient to write a forgiving letter to target of anger as step toward letting go of anger. Process letter in session.

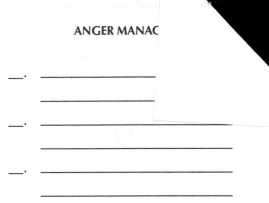

__. _____
     _____

__. _____
     _____
     _____

__. _____
     _____

DIAGNOSTIC SUGGESTIONS

Axis I: 312.43   Intermittent Explosive Disorder
              296.xx   Bipolar I Disorder
              296.89   Bipolar II Disorder
              312.8   Conduct Disorder
              310.1   Personality Change Due to (Axis III Disorder)
              309.81   Posttraumatic Stress Disorder

              _____   _____

Axis II: 301.83   Borderline Personality Disorder
              301.7   Antisocial Personality Disorder
              301.0   Paranoid Personality Disorder
              301.81   Narcissistic Personality Disorder
              301.9   Personality Disorder NOS

              _____   _____
              _____   _____

ANTISOCIAL BEHAVIOR

BEHAVIORAL DEFINITIONS

1. An adolescent history of consistent rule-breaking, lying, physical aggression, disrespect for others and their property, stealing, and/or substance abuse resulting in frequent confrontation with authority.
2. Consistent pattern of blaming others for what happens to him/her.
3. Refusal to follow rules with the attitude that they apply to others, not him/her.
4. History of reckless behaviors that reflect a lack of regard for self or others and show a high need for excitement, having fun, and living on the edge.
5. Little regard for truth as reflected in a pattern of consistently lying to and/or conning others.
6. Pattern of sexual promiscuity; has never been totally monogamous in any relationship for a year and does not take responsibility for children.
7. Pattern of interacting in an irritable, aggressive, and/or argumentative way with authority figures.
8. Little or no remorse for hurtful behavior.
9. Verbal or physical fighting often initiated.
10. Failure to conform with social norms with respect to the law as shown by repeatedly performed antisocial acts that he/she may or may not have been arrested for (e.g., destroying property, stealing, or pursuing an illegal job).
11. Pattern of impulsive behaviors, such as moving often, traveling with no goal, or quitting a job without having another.
12. Inability to sustain behavior that would maintain consistent employment.
13. Failure to function as a consistently concerned and responsible parent.

—. _____
    _____
—. _____
    _____
—. _____
    _____

LONG-TERM GOALS

1. Become more responsible for behavior and keep behavior within the acceptable limits of the rules of society.
2. Develop and demonstrate a healthy sense of respect for social norms, the rights of others, and the need for honesty.
3. Improve method of relating to the world, especially authority figures; be more realistic, less defiant, and more socially sensitive.
4. Come to an understanding and acceptance of the need for limits and boundaries on behavior.
5. Accept responsibility for own actions, including apologizing for hurts and not blaming others.
6. Maintain consistent employment and demonstrate financial and emotional responsibility for children.

—. _____
    _____
—. _____
    _____
—. _____
    _____

SHORT-TERM OBJECTIVES

1. Admit to illegal and/or unethical behavior that has trampled on the law and/or rights and feelings of others. (1, 2)

THERAPEUTIC INTERVENTIONS

1. Explore the history of patient's pattern of illegal and/or unethical behavior and confront attempts at minimization, denial, or projection of blame.

2. Verbalize an understanding of the benefits for self and others of living within the laws and rules of society. (3, 4)

3. Make a commitment to live within the rules and laws of society. (4, 5, 6)

4. List relationships that have been broken because of disrespect, disloyalty, aggression, or dishonesty. (7, 8)

5. Acknowledge a pattern of self-centeredness in virtually all relationships. (8, 9)

6. Verbalize an understanding of the benefits for self and others of being honest and reliable. (10, 11)

7. Make a commitment to be honest and reliable. (10, 11, 12)

8. Verbalize an understanding of the benefits to self and others of being empathetic and sensitive to the needs of others. (3, 13, 14)

9. List three actions that will be performed that will be acts of kindness and thoughtfulness toward others. (3, 15)

10. List those who deserve an apology for hurtful behaviors. (7, 8, 16, 17)

11. Indicate steps that will be taken to make amends or restitution for hurt caused to others. (16, 17, 18)

2. Review the consequences for self and others of the antisocial behavior.

3. Teach that the basis for all relationships is trust that the other person will treat one with respect and kindness.

4. Teach the need for lawfulness as the basis for trust which forestalls anarchy in society as a whole.

5. Solicit a commitment to live a prosocial, law-abiding lifestyle.

6. Emphasize the reality of negative consequences for patient if continued lawlessness is practiced.

7. Review relationships that have been lost due to antisocial attitudes and practices (e.g., disloyalty, dishonesty, aggression, etc.).

8. Confront the lack of sensitivity to the needs and feelings of others.

9. Point out the self-focused, me-first, look-out-for-number-one attitude that is reflected in the antisocial behavior.

10. Teach the value of honesty and reliability for self as the basis for trust and respect in all relationships and social approval.

11. Teach the positive effect that honesty and reliability have for others as they are not disappointed or hurt by lies and broken promises.

12. Verbally demonstrate an understanding of the rules and duties related to employment. (19)

13. Attend work reliably and treat supervisor and coworkers with respect. (20, 21)

14. Verbalize the obligations of parenthood that have been ignored. (22, 23)

15. State a plan to meet responsibilities toward children. (23, 24)

16. Decrease statements of blame of others or circumstances for own behavior, thoughts, and feelings. (1, 17, 22, 25, 26)

17. Increase statements of accepting responsibility for own behavior. (16, 17, 18, 24, 27)

18. Describe instances in childhood of emotional, verbal, and/or physical abuse. (26, 28)

19. Verbalize an understanding of how childhood experiences of pain and aggression have led to an imitative pattern of self-focused protection and aggression toward others. (28, 29)

20. Verbalize a desire to forgive perpetrators of childhood abuse. (28, 29, 30)

21. Verbalize fears associated with trusting others. (28, 29, 31)

12. Ask patient to make a commitment to be honest and reliable.

13. Attempt to sensitize patient to his/her lack of empathy for others by revisiting consequences of behavior on others. Use role reversal techniques.

14. Confront patient when rude or not being respectful of others and their boundaries.

15. Assist patient in listing three actions that he/she will perform as acts of service or kindness for others.

16. Assist patient in identifying those who have been hurt by his/her antisocial behavior.

17. Teach the value of apologizing for hurt caused as a means of accepting responsibility for behavior and developing sensitivity to the feelings of others.

18. Encourage a commitment to specific steps that will be taken to apologize, make restitution to those who have suffered from patient's hurtful behaviors.

19. Review the rules and expectations that must govern behavior at the work setting.

20. Monitor attendance at work and reinforce reliability as well as respect for authority.

22. Practice trusting a significant other with disclosure of personal feelings. (17, 29, 32)

23. Report on the experience of being more trusting in self-disclosure. (31, 32, 33)

—. _____
   _____

—. _____
   _____

—. _____
   _____

21. Ask patient to make a list of behaviors and attitudes that must be modified in order to decrease his/her conflict with authorities. Process list with therapist.

22. Confront patient's avoidance of responsibilities toward his/her children.

23. Assist patient in listing the behaviors that are required to be a responsible, nurturant, consistently reliable parent.

24. Develop a plan with patient that will begin to implement behaviors of a responsible parent.

25. Confront patient when making blaming statements or failing to take responsibility for actions, thoughts, or feelings.

26. Explore with patient reasons for blaming others for own actions.

27. Give verbal positive feedback to patient when he/she is taking responsibility for his/her own behavior.

28. Explore history of abuse, neglect, or abandonment in childhood.

29. Point out that the pattern of emotional detachment in relationships and self-focused behavior is related to a dysfunctional attempt to protect self from pain.

30. Teach the value of forgiveness of the perpetrators of hurt versus holding on to

hurt and rage, using the
hurt as an excuse to con-
tinue antisocial practices.

31. Explore fears associated
with placing trust in others.

32. Identify some personal
thoughts and feelings that
could be shared with a significant other as a means of
beginning to demonstrate
trust in someone.

33. Process the experience of
patient making self a little
vulnerable by self-disclosing
to someone.

___. _____

_____

___. _____

_____

___. _____

_____

DIAGNOSTIC SUGGESTIONS

Axis I:	303.90	Alcohol Dependence
	304.20	Cocaine Dependence
	304.89	Polysubstance Dependence
	309.3	Adjustment Disorder with Disturbance of Conduct
	312.8	Conduct Disorder
	312.34	Intermittent Explosive Disorder
	_____	_____
	_____	_____
Axis II:	301.7	Antisocial Personality Disorder
	301.81	Narcissistic Personality Disorder
	_____	_____
	_____	_____

ANXIETY

BEHAVIORAL DEFINITIONS

1. Excessive and persistent daily worry about several life circumstances that has no factual or logical basis.
2. Symptoms of motor tension such as restlessness, tiredness, shakiness, or muscle tension.
3. Symptoms of autonomic hyperactivity such as palpitations, shortness of breath, dry mouth, trouble swallowing, nausea, or diarrhea.
4. Symptoms of hypervigilance such as feeling constantly on edge, concentration difficulties, trouble falling or staying asleep, and general state of irritability.

__. _____
_____

__. _____
_____

__. _____
_____

LONG-TERM GOALS

1. Reduce overall level, frequency, and intensity of the anxiety so that daily functioning is not impaired.
2. Stabilize anxiety level while increasing ability to function on a daily basis.
3. Resolve the core conflict that is the source of anxiety.
4. Enhance ability to handle effectively the full variety of life's anxieties.

—. _____
    _____
—. _____
    _____
—. _____
    _____

SHORT-TERM OBJECTIVES

1. Tell the story of the anxiety complete with ways he/she has attempted to resolve it and the suggestions others have given. (1, 2)

2. Identify major life conflicts from the past and present. (3, 4)

3. Complete anxiety homework exercises that identify cognitive distractions that generate anxious feelings. (5)

4. Complete physical evaluation for medications. (6)

5. Take medications as prescribed and report any side effects to appropriate professionals. (7)

6. Develop appropriate relaxation and diversion activities to decrease level of anxiety. (8, 9, 10)

7. Increase daily social and vocational involvement. (11)

8. Identify how worries are irrational. (12, 13)

THERAPEUTIC INTERVENTIONS

1. Build a level of trust with patient and create a supportive environment which will facilitate a description of his/her fears.

2. Probe with questions (see *Anxiety Disorders and Phobias* by Beck and Emery) which require the patient to produce evidence of the anxiety and logical reasons for it being present.

3. Ask patient to develop and process a list of key past and present life conflicts.

4. Assist patient in becoming aware of key unresolved life conflicts and in starting to work toward their resolution.

5. Assign patient to complete, and process with therapist, the anxiety section exercises in *Ten Days to Self-Esteem!* (Burns).

6. Make a referral to a physician for a medication consultation.

9. Increase understanding of beliefs and messages that produce worry and anxiety. (13, 14)

10. Verbalize insight into how past traumatic experiences are causing anxiety in present unrelated circumstances. (15)

11. Decrease daily level of anxiety by developing positive self-talk. (16)

12. Implement thought-stopping technique to interrupt anxiety-producing thoughts. (17)

13. List the advantages and disadvantages of the anxiety. (18)

14. Verbalize positive principles that reduce anxious thoughts. (19)

15. Verbalize alternative positive views of reality that are incompatible with anxiety-producing views. (20)

16. Identify an anxiety coping mechanism that has been successful in the past and increase its use. (21)

17. Utilize paradoxical intervention to reduce anxiety response. (22)

—. _____
_____

—. _____
_____

—. _____
_____

7. Monitor medication compliance, side effects, and effectiveness. Confer with physician regularly.

8. Train in guided imagery for anxiety relief.

9. Utilize biofeedback techniques to facilitate relaxation skills.

10. Assign or allow patient to choose a chapter in *Relaxation and Stress Reduction Workbook* (Davis, Eshelman, and McKay), then work with him/her to implement the chosen technique.

11. Assist patient in developing coping strategies (e.g., increased social involvement, obtaining employment, or physical exercise) for his/her anxiety.

12. Assist patient in developing an awareness of the irrational nature of his/her fears.

13. Analyze the fear with the patient by examining the probability of the negative expectation occurring, so what if it happens, ability to control it, the worst possible outcome, and the patient's ability to accept it. (See *Anxiety Disorders and Phobias* by Beck and Emery.)

14. Explore cognitive messages that mediate anxiety response and retrain in adaptive cognitions.

15. Reinforce insights into past emotional issues and present anxiety.

16. Help patient develop reality-based, positive cognitive messages that will increase self-confidence in coping with irrational fears.

17. Teach patient to implement a thought-stopping technique that cognitively interferes with obsessions by thinking of a stop sign and then a pleasant scene. Monitor and encourage patient's use of technique in daily life between sessions.

18. Ask patient to complete and process with therapist "Cost-Benefit Analysis" exercise (see *Ten Days to Self-Esteem!* by Burns) in which he/she lists the advantages and disadvantages of the negative thought, fear, or anxiety.

19. Read and process a fable from *Friedman's Fables* (Friedman) that pertains to anxiety with the patient.

20. Reframe the fear or anxiety by offering another way of looking at it, various alternatives, or by enlarging the perspective.

21. Utilize a brief solution-focused therapy approach in which the patient is probed to find a time or situation in his/her life when he/she handled the specific anxiety or an anxiety in general.

Clearly focus the approach he/she used and then encourage the patient to increase the use of this. Monitor and modify the solution as required.

22. Develop a paradoxical intervention (see *Ordeal Therapy* by Haley) in which the patient is encouraged to have the problem (e.g., anxiety) and then schedule that anxiety to occur at specific intervals each day in a specific way and for a defined length of time. It is best to have it happen at a time of day/night when the patient would be clearly wanting to do something else.

__. _____
   _____
__. _____
   _____
__. _____
   _____

DIAGNOSTIC SUGGESTIONS

Axis I:	300.02	Generalized Anxiety Disorder
	300.00	Anxiety Disorder NOS
	309.24	Adjustment Disorder with Anxiety
	_____	_____
	_____	_____

ATTENTION DEFICIT
DISORDER (ADD)—ADULT

BEHAVIORAL DEFINITIONS

1. Childhood history of Attention Deficit Disorder (ADD) that was either diagnosed or later concluded from by the symptoms of behavioral problems at school, impulsivity, overexcitability, temper outbursts, and lack of concentration.
2. Unable to concentrate or pay attention to things of low interest, even when those things are important to his/her life.
3. Easily distracted and drawn from task at hand.
4. Restless and fidgety; unable to be sedentary for more than a short time.
5. Impulsive; has an easily observable pattern of acting first, thinking later.
6. Rapid mood swings and mood lability within short spans of time.
7. Disorganized in most areas of his/her life.
8. Starts many projects but rarely finishes any.
9. Has a "low boiling point and a short fuse."
10. Exhibits low stress tolerance; is easily frustrated, hassled or upset.
11. Chronic low self-esteem.
12. Tendency toward addictive behaviors.

__. _____

_____

__. _____

_____

__. _____

_____

LONG-TERM GOALS

1. Reduce impulsive actions while increasing concentration and focus on low-interest activities.
2. Reduce ADD behavioral interference in daily life.
3. Acceptance of ADD as a chronic issue and in need of continuing medication treatment.
4. Sustain attention and concentration for consistently longer periods of time.
5. Achieve a satisfactory level of balance, structure, and intimacy to personal life.

___. _____

_____

___. _____

_____

___. _____

_____

SHORT-TERM OBJECTIVES

1. Cooperate with and complete psychological testing. (1, 2, 7)

2. Cooperate with and complete psychiatric evaluation. (3)

3. Comply with all recommendations of the psychiatric and/or psychological evaluations. (2, 4, 7)

4. Take medication as prescribed on a regular, consistent basis. (5, 6)

5. Identify specific benefits of taking prescribed medications on a long-term basis. (8, 9, 10)

THERAPEUTIC INTERVENTIONS

1. Arrange for the administration of psychological testing to establish or rule out Attention-Deficit/ Hyperactivity Disorder (ADHD).

2. Process the results of psychological testing with patient to aid understanding and answer any questions which he/she may have.

3. Arrange for a psychiatric evaluation to make medication recommendations.

4. Process results and recommendations of psychiatric evaluation with patient and answer any questions that may arise.

6. Identify the specific ADD behaviors that cause self the most difficulty. (11, 12, 13)

7. Apply problem-solving skills to specific ADD behaviors that are interfering with daily functioning. (14, 15)

8. Utilize cognitive strategies to curb impulsive behavior. (16)

9. Implement a specific, time-limited period of indulging impulses that are not self-destructive. (17)

10. Use "time out" to remove self from situations and think about behavioral reaction alternatives and their consequences. (18)

11. Implement relaxation procedures to reduce tension and physical restlessness. (19)

12. Reward self when problem behaviors (e.g., impulsivity, inattention, etc.) are replaced with positive alternatives. (20)

13. Use lists, sticky notes, and daily routines to decrease effects of inattention. (21)

14. Cooperate with brainwave biofeedback to improve impulse control and reduce distractibility. (22, 23)

15. Introduce behaviors into life that improve health (e.g., increased exercise) and/or serve others (e.g., community service). (24, 25)

5. Monitor and evaluate medication compliance and the effectiveness of the medications on the patient's level of functioning.

6. Confer with psychiatrist on regular basis regarding effectiveness of the medication regime.

7. Conduct a conjoint session with significant others and patient to present the results of psychological and psychiatric evaluations. Answer any questions they may have and solicit their support in dealing with patient's condition.

8. Ask patient to make a "pros and cons" spreadsheet regarding staying on medications after doing well. Process sheet with therapist.

9. Encourage and support patient in remaining on medications and warmly but firmly confront thoughts of discontinuing when they surface.

10. Assign patient to list the positive effects that have occurred for him/her since starting on medication.

11. Assist patient in identifying the specific behaviors that cause him/her the most difficulty.

12. Review the results of psychological testing and/or psychiatric evaluation again with patient to assist

16. List the negative consequences of the ADD prob-
lematic behavior. (26)

17. Attend an ADD support
group. (27)

18. Use a "coach" who has been
trained by therapist to increase organization and
task focus. (28, 29)

19. Report improved listening
skills without defensive-
ness. (30)

20. Read material that is infor-
mative regarding ADD to
gain knowledge about the
condition. (31)

21. Decrease statements and
feelings of negativity regarding self and life. (32)

22. Have significant other attend an ADD support group
to increase his/her understanding of the condition.
(33)

23. Attend a communication
improvement group with
significant other. (34)

24. Verbalize expectations
partners have for each
other. (35)

25. Report improved communication and feelings of trust
between self and significant
other. (34, 35, 36, 37)

26. Develop signals between
partners to act as a warning
system to indicate when
problematic behaviors are
escalating. (38)

in identifying or in affirm-
ing his/her choice of a most
problematic behavior(s) to
address.

13. Ask patient to have extended family members and
close colaterals complete a
ranking of the three behaviors they see as interfering
the most with his/her daily
functioning (e.g., mood
swings, temper outbursts,
impulsivity, restlessness,
easily stressed, short attention span, never completes
projects, etc.).

14. Teach (or expand) patient's
problem-solving skills (i.e.,
identify problem, brain-
storm all possible options,
evaluate each option, select
best option, implement
course of action, and evaluate results).

15. Assign problem-solving
homework to patient spe-
cific to identified behavior
(i.e., impulse control, anger
outbursts, mood swings,
staying on task, attentive-
ness). Process the com-
pleted assignment and give
appropriate feedback to
patient.

16. Teach patient the self-
control strategies of "stop,
listen, think, act" and
"problem-solving self-talk."
Role-play these techniques
to improve skill level.

17. Structure a "blow out" time
each week when patient can
do whatever he/she likes to

__. _____
    _____
__. _____
    _____
__. _____
    _____

do that is not self-destructive (e.g., blast themselves with music, gorge on ice cream, etc.).

18. Train patient to use "time-out" intervention in which he/she settles down by going away from the situation and calming down to think about behavioral alternatives and their consequences.

19. Instruct patient in various relaxation techniques (e.g., deep breathing, meditation, guided imagery, etc.) and encourage patient to use daily or when stress increases.

20. Design and implement a self-administered reward system to reinforce and encourage patient's decreased impulsiveness, loss of temper, inattentiveness, and so on.

21. Assist patient in utilizing external structure such as lists, reminders, files, and/or daily rituals to reduce effects of inattention and forgetfulness.

22. Refer for or administer brainwave biofeedback to improve attention span, impulse control, and mood regulation.

23. Encourage the patient to transfer the biofeedback training skills of relaxation and cognitive focusing to everyday situations (e.g., home, work, and social).

24. Direct patient toward healthy addictions such as exercise, volunteer work, or community service.

25. After clearance from patient's personal physician, refer patient to a physical fitness trainer who can design an aerobic exercise routine for the patient.

26. Assign patient to make a list of negative consequences either that he/she has experienced or that could result from the problematic behavior. Process list with therapist.

27. Refer to a specific group therapy for adults with ADD to increase patient's understanding of ADD, to boost his/her self-esteem, and to receive feedback from others.

28. Direct patient to pick a "coach" who is a friend or colleague to assist him/her in getting organized and staying on task and to give encouragement support. (See *Driven to Distraction* by Hallowell and Raty.)

29. Instruct coach in HOPE technique (i.e., Help, Obligations, Plans, and Encouragement) as described in *Driven to Distraction* (Hallowell and Raty).

30. Use role-playing and modeling to teach patient how to listen and accept feedback from others regarding his/her behavior.

31. Ask patient to read *Driven to Distraction* (Hallowell and Raty), *The Hyperactive Child, Adolescent and Adult* (Wender), *Putting On The Brakes* (Quinn and Stern); and/or *You Mean I'm Not Lazy, Stupid or Crazy* (Kelly and Ramundo). Process reading with therapist.

32. Conduct conjoint sessions in which positive aspects of the relationship, patient, and significant other are identified and affirmed.

33. Educate significant other on ADD and encourage him/her to attend a support group.

34. Refer patient and significant other to a skill-based marriage/relationship seminar (e.g., PREP, Marriage Encounter, Engaged Encounter, etc.) to improve communication and conflict resolution skills.

35. Ask patient and significant other to list the expectations they have for the relationship and each other. Process list in conjoint session with focus on identifying how expectations can be met and how realistic they are.

36. Assist patient and significant other in removing blocks in communication and in developing new communication skills.

37. Assign patient and significant other to schedule a specific time each day to

spend together communi-
cating, expressing affection,
having fun, or talking
through problems. Move
assignment toward becom-
ing a daily ritual.

38. Assist patient and significant other in developing a
signal system as a means of
giving feedback when con-
flict behaviors begin to
escalate.

__. _____
   _____

__. _____
   _____

__. _____
   _____

DIAGNOSTIC SUGGESTIONS

Axis I:	314.00	Attention-Deficit/Hyperactivity Disorder, Predominately Inattentive Type
	314.01	Attention-Deficit/Hyperactivity Disorder, Predominately Hyperactivity-Impulsive Type
	314.9	Attention-Deficit/Hyperactivity Disorder NOS
	296.xx	Bipolar I Disorder
	301.13	Cyclothymic Disorder
	296.90	Mood Disorder NOS
	312.30	Impulse Control Disorder NOS
	303.90	Alcohol Dependence
	305.00	Alcohol Abuse
	304.30	Cannabis Dependence
	305.20	Cannabis Abuse
	_____	_____
	_____	_____

BORDERLINE PERSONALITY

BEHAVIORAL DEFINITIONS

1. Extreme emotional reactivity (anger, anxiety, or depression) under minor stress that usually does not last more than a few hours to a few days.
2. A pattern of intense, chaotic interpersonal relationships.
3. Marked identity disturbance.
4. Impulsive behaviors that are potentially self-damaging.
5. Recurrent suicidal gestures, threats, or self-mutilating behavior.
6. Chronic feelings of emptiness and boredom.
7. Frequent eruptions of intense, inappropriate anger.
8. Easily feels that others are treating him/her unfairly or that they can't be trusted.
9. Analyzes most issues in simple terms of right and wrong (e.g., black/white, trustworthy/deceitful) without regard for extenuating circumstances or complex situations.
10. Becomes very anxious with any hint of perceived abandonment in a relationship.

LONG-TERM GOALS

1. Develop and demonstrate coping skills to deal with mood swings.
2. Develop the ability to control impulses.
3. Learn and demonstrate strategies to deal with dysphoric moods.
4. Replace dichotomous thinking with ability to tolerate ambiguity and complexity in people and issues.
5. Develop and demonstrate anger management skills.
6. Learn and practice interpersonal relationship skills.
7. Reduce the frequency of self-damaging behaviors (such as substance abuse, reckless driving, sexual acting out, binge eating, or suicidal behaviors).

__. _____

_____

__. _____

_____

__. _____

_____

SHORT-TERM OBJECTIVES	THERAPEUTIC INTERVENTIONS
1. Verbalize the situations that can easily trigger feelings of fear, depression, and anger. (1)	1. Explore the situations that trigger feelings of fear, depression, and anger.
2. Write a daily journal of feelings and the circumstances that triggered those feelings. (2)	2. Assign patient to record a daily journal of feelings along with the circumstances that he/she was reacting to.
3. Identify the negative cognitive interpretation patterns that mediate the intense negative emotions. (3, 4)	3. Identify the distorted schemas and related automatic thoughts that mediate anxiety response.
4. Verbalize realistic, positive self-talk to replace distorted negative messages. (4, 5, 6)	4. Require patient to keep a daily record of self-defeating thoughts (thoughts of hopelessness, helplessness, worthlessness, catastrophiz-
5. Record and report instances of implementing positive	

self-talk and constructive automatic thoughts; include rewarding consequences. (6, 7)

6. List some negative consequences to self and others of self-defeating impulsive behaviors. (8)

7. Verbalize an understanding of the impulse control strategy of "stop, look, listen, and think." (9)

8. Record and report instances of implementing "Stop, Look, Listen, and Think" as an impulse control strategy. (9, 10)

9. Utilize cognitive methods to control impulsive behavior. (9, 11)

10. Practice deep muscle relaxation and deep breathing exercises. (12)

11. Record and report instances of using relaxation techniques to manage intense feelings and control impulsive reactive behavior. (13)

12. Practice assertiveness skills. (14, 15)

13. Identify situations where assertiveness has been implemented and describe the consequences. (16)

14. Implement the use of "I messages" to communicate feelings without aggression. (17, 18)

15. Verbalize instances of abuse, neglect, or abandonment in childhood. (19)

ing, negatively predicti the future, etc.), challenge each thought for accuracy, then replace each dysfunctional thought with one that is positive and self-enhancing.

5. Train in revising core schema using cognitive restructuring techniques.

6. Reinforce positive, realistic cognitive self-talk that mediates a sense of peace.

7. Assign patient to record instances of successfully using revised, constructive cognitive patterns. Process and reinforce positive consequences.

8. Assign patient to list destructive consequences to self and others of impulsive behavior.

9. Teach the patient mediational and self-control strategies (i.e., "stop, look, listen, and think") to delay gratification and inhibit impulses.

10. Assign patient to record instances of successfully implementing "stop, look, listen, and think" to control reactive impulses.

11. Teach patient cognitive methods (thought stoppage, thought substitution, reframing, etc.) for gaining and improving control over impulsive actions.

16. Verbalize the effect that childhood experiences of abuse, neglect, or abandonment has upon possessiveness in relationships and sensitivity to a hint of loss of commitment by others to relationship with self. (20, 21)

17. List coping strategies to deal with fear of abandonment. (22)

18. Initiate enjoyable activities that can be done alone or are not dependent on someone else to do them with. Report feeling comfortable being alone or independent. (4, 6, 23, 24)

19. Cooperate with a referral to a physician to evaluate the need for psychotropic medication to stabilize mood. (25)

20. Take medication as prescribed and report as to effectiveness and side effects. (26)

21. Describe the history and nature of self-mutilating behavior. (27)

22. Verbalize the intense feelings that motivate self-mutilating behavior and how those feelings are relieved by such behavior. (19, 21, 28)

23. Verbalize the history of suicidal gestures and the feelings associated with them. (29)

12. Using relaxation techniques such as progressive relaxation, self-hypnosis, or biofeedback; teach the patient how to relax completely; then have the patient relax whenever he/she feels uncomfortable.

13. Ask patient to record instances of using relaxation techniques to cope with stress rather than reacting with anger. Reinforce successful implementation of this coping skill.

14. Use role-playing, modeling, and behavioral rehearsal to teach assertiveness (versus passivity and aggressiveness).

15. Refer patient to an assertiveness training group.

16. Review implementation of assertiveness and feelings about it as well as the consequences of it.

17. Use modeling, role-playing, and behavioral rehearsal to teach the use of "I messages" to communicate feelings directly (i.e., I feel . . . When you . . . I would prefer it if you . . .).

18. Reinforce the use of "I messages" in place of aggressiveness or possessiveness when feeling threatened.

19. Explore instances of abuse, neglect, or emotional/physical abandonment in childhood. Process the feelings associated with these experiences.

24. Verbalize a promise (as part of a self-mutilation and suicide prevention contract) to contact the therapist or some other emergency helpline if a serious urge toward self-harm arises. (30, 31)

25. Terminate all self-mutilation behavior. (21, 30, 32)

26. Identify instances where people were judged in black and white terms. (33, 35)

27. List negative consequences of judging people so rigidly and harshly. (34)

28. Verbalize weaknesses or faults of those who have been judged to be perfect and strengths or assets of those people who have been judged to be evil, worthless, and deceitful. (35, 36)

__. _____
_____
__. _____
_____
__. _____
_____

20. Point out the destructive effect of overcontrol of others and angry resentment when others pull back from relationship. Encourage separation of helpless, desperate feelings of the past from current relationships.

21. Reinforce insight into the effect of childhood experiences on current urges to react with rage.

22. Teach patient to use coping strategies (e.g., delay of reaction, "stop, look, listen, and plan," relaxation and deep breathing techniques, "I messages," expanded social network versus few intense relationships) to deal with fear of abandonment.

23. Explore patient's automatic thoughts associated with being alone.

24. Encourage patient to break pattern of avoiding being alone by initiating activities without a companion (e.g., starting a hobby; doing exercise; attending lectures, concerts, movies; reading a book; taking a class).

25. Refer patient to a physician for medication evaluation.

26. Monitor and evaluate patient's medication compliance and the effectiveness of the medication on the level of functioning.

27. Probe nature and history of patient's self-mutilating behavior.

28. Interpret the self-mutilation as an expression of the rage and helplessness that could not be expressed as a child victim of emotional abandonment or abuse.

29. Assess the suicidal gestures as to triggers, frequency, seriousness, secondary gain, and onset.

30. Elicit a promise from the patient that he/she will initiate contact with the therapist or a helpline if the suicidal urge becomes strong and before any self-injurious behavior.

31. Provide the patient with an emergency helpline telephone number that is available 24 hours a day.

32. Encourage patient to express feelings directly using assertive "I messages" rather than indirectly through self-mutilating behavior.

33. Ask patient to examine his/her style of evaluating people, especially in regard to his/her dichotomous thinking.

34. Teach the alienating consequences of judging people harshly and impulsively.

35. Challenge the patient in understanding how dichotomous thinking leads to feelings of interpersonal mistrust, helping him/her to see positive *and* negative traits in all people.

36. Use role reversal and modeling to assist patient in seeing positive and negative qualities in all people.

—. _____

_____

—. _____

_____

—. _____

_____

DIAGNOSTIC SUGGESTIONS

Axis I: 300.4   Dysthymic Disorder
296.3x   Major Depressive Disorder, Recurrent

_____   _____

Axis II: 301.83   Borderline Personality Disorder
301.9   Personality Disorder NOS

_____   _____

_____   _____

CHEMICAL DEPENDENCE

BEHAVIORAL DEFINITIONS

1. Consistent use of alcohol or other mood-altering drugs until high, intoxicated, or passed out.
2. Inability to stop or cut down use of mood-altering drug once started, despite the verbalized desire to do so and the negative consequences continued use brings.
3. Blood work that reflects the results of a pattern of heavy substance use, for example, elevated liver enzymes.
4. Denial that chemical dependence is a problem despite direct feedback from spouse, relatives, friends, and employers that the use of the substance is negatively affecting them and others.
5. Amnesiac blackouts have occurred when abusing alcohol.
6. Continued drug and/or alcohol use despite experiencing persistent or recurring physical, legal, vocational, social, or relationship problems that are directly caused by the use of the substance.
7. Increased tolerance for the drug as there is the need to use more to become intoxicated or to attain the desired effect.
8. Physical symptoms, that is, shaking, seizures, nausea, headaches, sweating, anxiety, insomnia, and/or depression, when withdrawing from the substance.
9. Suspension of important social, recreational, or occupational activities because they interfere with using.
10. Large time investment in activities to obtain the substance, to use it, or to recover from its effects.
11. Consumption of substance in greater amounts and for longer periods than intended.
12. Continued use of mood-altering chemical after being told by a physician that it is causing health problems.

—. _____
_____
—. _____
_____
—. _____
_____

LONG-TERM GOALS

1. Accept chemical dependence and begin to actively participate in a recovery program.
2. Establish a sustained recovery, free from the use of all mood-altering substances.
3. Establish and maintain total abstinence while increasing knowledge of the disease and the process of recovery.
4. Acquire the necessary skills to maintain long-term sobriety from all mood-altering substances and live a life free of chemicals.
5. Improve quality of life by maintaining an ongoing abstinence from all mood-altering chemicals.
6. Withdraw from mood-altering substance, stabilize physically and emotionally, and then establish a supportive recovery plan.

—. _____
_____
—. _____
_____
—. _____
_____

SHORT-TERM OBJECTIVES

1. Describe the amount, frequency, and history of substance abuse. (1, 3)
2. Identify the negative consequences of drug and/or alcohol abuse. (1, 2, 3, 4, 13)

THERAPEUTIC INTERVENTIONS

1. Gather a complete drug/alcohol history including amount and pattern of use, signs and symptoms of use, and negative life consequences (social, legal, familial, and vocational)

3. Make verbal "I" statements that reflect acknowledgment and acceptance of chemical dependence. (5, 6, 7)

4. Decrease the level of denial around using as evidenced by fewer statements about minimizing amount of use and its negative impact on life. (2, 4, 6, 7)

5. Verbalize increased knowledge of alcoholism and the process of recovery. (6, 8)

6. Verbalize an understanding of personality, social, and family factors that foster chemical dependence. (9, 10, 11)

7. Describe childhood experience of alcohol abuse by immediate and extended family members. (11)

8. Review extended family alcohol use history and verbalize an acceptance of a genetic component to chemical dependence. (11, 12)

9. Obtain a medical examination to evaluate the effects of chemical dependence. (13)

10. Identify the ways being sober could positively impact life. (14)

11. State changes that will be made in social relationships to support recovery. (15, 16)

resulting from client's chemical dependence.

2. Ask client to make a list of the ways substance abuse has negatively impacted his/her life and process it with therapist.

3. Administer the Alcohol Severity Index, and process the results with the client.

4. Assign client to ask two or three people who are close to him/her to write a letter to therapist in which they identify how they saw client's chemical dependence negatively impacting his/her life.

5. Assign client to complete a First Step paper and then process it with either group, sponsor, or therapist to receive feedback.

6. Require client to attend didactic lectures related to chemical dependence and the process of recovery. Then ask client to identify in writing several key points attained from each lecture for further processing with therapist.

7. Model and reinforce statements that reflect acceptance of chemical dependence and its destructive consequences for self and others.

8. Assign client to read article/pamphlet on the disease concept of alcoholism and select several key ideas to discuss with therapist.

12. List recreational and social activities (and places) that will replace substance abuse related activities. (16, 17)

13. Identify constructive projects that will be accomplished now that time and energy are available in sobriety. (16, 18)

14. Agree to make amends to significant others who have been hurt by the life dominated by substance abuse. (16, 19)

15. Identify the positive impact that sobriety will have on intimate and family relationships. (16, 20)

16. Verbalize how living situation contributes to chemical dependence and acts as a hindrance to recovery. (10, 21, 22)

17. State the need for a more stable, healthy living situation that will support recovery. (22, 23)

18. Make arrangements to terminate current living situation and move to a place more conducive to recovery. (23, 24)

19. Write a goodbye letter to drug of choice telling it why it must go. (25)

20. Sign an abstinence contract and verbalize feelings of fear, grief, or reluctance associated with signing. (26)

9. Assess client's intellectual, personality, and cognitive functioning as to his/her contribution to chemical dependence.

10. Investigate situational stress factors that may foster client's chemical dependence.

11. Probe client's family history for chemical dependence patterns and relate these to client's use.

12. Explore extended family chemical dependence history and relate this to a genetic vulnerability for client to develop chemical dependence also.

13. Refer client for thorough physical examination to determine any physical effects of chemical dependence.

14. Ask client to make and process a list of how being sober could positively impact life.

15. Review the negative influence of continuing old alcohol-related friendships ("drinking buddies") and assist client in making a plan to develop new sober friendships.

16. Assist the client in developing insight into life changes needed in order to maintain long-term sobriety.

17. Assist client in planning social and recreational activities that are free from association with substance abuse.

21. Develop a written aftercare plan that will support the maintenance of long-term sobriety. (16, 17, 18, 27, 30)

22. Identify sources of ongoing support in maintaining sobriety. (28, 29, 30)

23. Meet with an Alcoholics Anonymous/Narcotics Anonymous (AA/NA) member to gain information about the role of AA/NA in recovery. (29)

24. Attend AA/NA meetings on a regular basis as frequently as necessary to support sobriety. (30)

25. Identify potential relapse triggers and develop strategies for constructively dealing with each trigger. (6, 10, 15, 17, 31, 32)

—. _____
   _____

—. _____
   _____

—. _____
   _____

18. Plan household or work-related projects that can be accomplished to build self-esteem now that sobriety affords time and energy for such constructive activity.

19. Discuss the negative effects substance abuse has had on family, friends, and work relationships and encourage a plan to make amends for such hurt.

20. Assist client in identifying positive changes that will be made in family relationships during recovery.

21. Evaluate the role of client's living situation in fostering a pattern of chemical dependence.

22. Assign client to write a list of negative influences for chemical dependence inherent in his/her current living situation.

23. Encourage a plan for a change in living situation that will foster recovery.

24. Reinforce a positive change in living situation.

25. Direct patient to write a good-bye letter to drug of choice; read it and process related feelings with therapist.

26. Develop an abstinence contract with patient regarding the use of his/her drug of choice. Then process the

emotional impact of this contract with therapist.

27. Assign and review patient's written aftercare plan to ensure it is adequate to maintain sobriety.

28. Explore with patient the positive support system personally available in sobriety and discuss ways to develop and reinforce a positive support system.

29. Assign patient to meet with an Alcoholics Anonymous/ Narcotics Anonymous (AA/NA) member who has been working the Twelve-Step program for several years and find out specifically how the program has helped him/her stay sober. Afterward, process the meeting with therapist.

30. Recommend patient attend AA or NA meetings and report to therapist the impact of the meetings.

31. Help patient develop an awareness of relapse triggers and alternative ways of effectively handling them.

32. Recommend the patient read *Staying Sober: A Guide to Relapse Prevention* (Gorski and Miller) and *The Staying Sober Workbook* (Gorski).

—. _____
_____
—. _____
_____
—. _____
_____

DIAGNOSTIC SUGGESTIONS

Axis I: 303.90   Alcohol Dependence
305.00   Alcohol Abuse
304.30   Cannabis Dependence
305.20   Cannabis Abuse
304.20   Cocaine Dependence
305.60   Cocaine Abuse
304.80   Polysubstance Dependence
291.2   Alcohol-Induced Persisting Dementia
291.1   Alcohol-Induced Persisting Amnestic Disorder
V71.01   Adult Antisocial Behavior
300.4   Dysthymic Disorder
312.34   Intermittent Explosive Disorder
309.81   Posttraumatic Stress Disorder
304.10   Sedative, Hypnotic, or Anxiolytic Dependence
_____   _____
_____   _____

Axis II: 301.7   Antisocial Personality Disorder
_____   _____
_____   _____

CHEMICAL DEPENDENCE—RELAPSE

BEHAVIORAL DEFINITIONS

1. Inability to remain abstinent from mood-altering drugs after receiving treatment for substance abuse.
2. Inability to stay sober even though attending Alcoholics Anonymous (AA) meetings regularly.
3. Relapse into abuse of mood-altering substances after a substantial period of sobriety.
4. Chronic pattern of periods of sobriety (6 months plus) followed by a relapse, then reestablishing sobriety.

—. _____
   _____
—. _____
   _____
—. _____
   _____

LONG-TERM GOALS

1. Establish a consistently alcohol/drug–free lifestyle.
2. Develop an understanding of personal pattern of relapse in order to help sustain long-term recovery.
3. Develop an increased awareness of physical relapse triggers and the coping strategies needed to effectively deal with them.
4. Achieve a quality of life that is substance free on a continuing basis.

___.   _____

      _____

___.   _____

      _____

___.   _____

      _____

SHORT-TERM OBJECTIVES

1. Verbalize a commitment to abstinence/sobriety. (1, 2)

2. Outline and implement a daily routine that is structured and includes AA involvement. (3, 4)

3. Reestablish ongoing relationships with people who are supportive of sobriety. (4, 5, 6)

4. Articulate people and places that must be avoided to maintain recovery. (7, 8, 9)

5. Verbalize feelings about the loss of sobriety. (10, 11)

6. Verbalize insights learned from talking and listening to successfully recovering chemically dependent people. (12)

7. Identify positive rewards associated with abstinence. (13, 14)

8. Complete medical assessment for Antabuse or antidepressant medications. (15)

9. Cooperate with acupuncture treatment to reduce

THERAPEUTIC INTERVENTIONS

1. Verbally discuss the specific behaviors, attitudes, and feelings that led up to the last relapse, focusing on triggers for the relapse. Obtain a clear, firm commitment to renewed sobriety.

2. Assess patient for ability to reestablish total abstinence and refer to more intense level of care if he/she is not able to detox and stay sober.

3. Teach the importance of structure and routine that have either been abandoned or never been present in patient's daily life and then assist patient in developing and implementing a balanced, structured daily routine.

4. Urge patient to attend AA without fail as a part of the routine structure of his/her life.

5. Assist patient in reuniting with AA sponsor.

6. Ask patient to find a second AA/NA sponsor who is opposite of primary sponsor

the urge to use mood-altering substances. (16, 17, 18)

10. Comply with medication recommendations as prescribed and report any side effects to the therapist and/or physician. (17, 18)

11. Verbally identify the specific behaviors, attitudes, and feelings that led up to the last relapse, focusing on triggers for the relapse. (8, 19, 20, 21, 22)

12. Meet with a spiritual leader to make progress on AA Steps 2, 3, and 5. (23)

13. Identify behavior patterns that will need to be changed to maintain sobriety. (8, 19, 24)

14. Demonstrate the ability to tolerate uncomfortable emotions that arise in group or individual sessions. (25, 26)

15. Articulate in writing a plan of actions for coping with uncomfortable feelings with steps up to and including contacting a sponsor. (5, 6, 26)

16. For each specific relapse trigger develop in writing two possible coping strategies. (8, 25, 26, 27, 28)

17. Implement assertiveness skills to communicate feelings directly. (28)

18. Verbally describe the family and relationship conflicts that played a role in triggering relapse. (29, 30)

(e.g., if primary is mainly supportive seek other who is more confrontive) and meet regularly with both sponsors on at least a weekly basis.

7. Assist patient in identifying the negative influence of people and situations that encourage relapse and ways to avoid them.

8. Assign patient to complete a relapse workbook (e.g., *The Staying Sober Workbook* by Gorski) and process it with therapist.

9. Assign patient to read a book or pamphlet on recovery. Select items from it that relate to him/her and process them with therapist.

10. Assist patient in expanding his/her ability to identify feelings, process them, and express them in a timely, healthy way.

11. Assign patient to read *The Golden Book of Resentment* (Father John Doe) or readings on resentment from *As Bill Sees It* (Bill Wilson), choose three key concepts he/she feels relate to him/her, and process each with therapist.

12. Ask patient to interview NA/AA members who have been sober for three or more years, focusing on what they specifically have done to accomplish this, and if they have relapsed, what they have done to get back

19. Have family or significant other verbalize an understanding of constructive actions they can take in reaction to patient's relapse and recovery. (30)

20. Participate in rituals that support recovery. (31)

21. Identify successful sober living strategies of the past. (32)

22. Verbalize principles to live by that will support sobriety. (33)

23. Develop written continuing aftercare plan with focus on coping with family and other stressors. (34, 35)

—. _____
   _____

—. _____
   _____

—. _____
   _____

on track to stay. Process findings with therapist.

13. Assist patient in identifying positive rewards of total abstinence.

14. Assign patient to complete and process with therapist a "Cost-Benefit Analysis" (see *Ten Days to Self-Esteem!* by Burns) on his/her return to substance abuse.

15. Refer patient to physician/ psychiatrist for an evaluation for Antabuse or antidepressant medication.

16. Refer patient to acupuncturist for treatment on a regular basis and monitor effectiveness.

17. Monitor patient for compliance with medication orders or other treatments and possible side effects as well as answer any questions he/she may have.

18. Confer with prescribing provider on a regular basis regarding the effectiveness of the treatment.

19. Ask patient to develop a list of behaviors, attitudes, and feelings that could have been involved in the relapse and process it with therapist.

20. Assign patient to do a focused autobiography from first attempt to get sober to present. Then read it to therapist for feedback as to triggers for relapse.

21. Ask patient to gather from significant other an observation list of patient's behavior or attitude prior to his/her returning to using. Process feedback in group therapy or in individual session.

22. Develop a symptom line with patient that looks at each relapse in terms of when it happened (i.e., time of year, dates and their significance) and what was occurring (i.e., in regard to self, spouse, family, work, or social activities).

23. Refer patient to a pastor, rabbi, priest or other spiritual leader with knowledge of substance abuse and recovery to work through any blocks regarding Steps 2 and 3 or to complete his/her Fifth Step.

24. Assign patient to read *Many Roads, One Journey: Moving Beyond the 12 Steps* (Kasl-Davis) or *Stage II Recovery* (Larsen) and process key ideas with therapist.

25. Teach patient various methods of stress reduction (i.e., meditation, deep breathing, etc.) and assist him/her in implementing into daily life.

26. Ask patient to develop a list of ways to handle uncomfortable feelings and process list with therapist.

27. Assist patient in developing two coping strategies for each identified trigger to relapse.

28. Assist patient in developing assertiveness techniques.

29. Conduct conjoint and/or family sessions which identify and resolve relationship stress that has served as a trigger for relapse.

30. Conduct sessions with spouse and/or significant other to educate them regarding relapse triggers and instruct them on how to be supportive of sobriety. Encourage them to attend Alanon on a regular basis.

31. Assist patient in developing and establishing rituals in life that will enhance sobriety and be a deterrent to relapse (e.g., receiving AA/NA coins, regular membership in a Step Study Group, coffee with sponsor at set date and time).

32. Utilize a brief solution-focused approach with patient to identify specific things he/she was doing when sobriety was going well and then select and direct patient to increase the use of the identified behaviors. Monitor and adjust direction as needed.

33. Read a fable or story such as "The Boy Who Lost His Way," "The Prodigal Son," or "Three Little Pigs" (see *Stories For the 3rd Ear,* by

Wallar), and process it with patient to identify key concepts connected to staying sober.

34. Ask patient to complete and process a relapse contract with significant other that identifies previous relapse-associated behaviors, attitudes, and emotions, coupling them with agreed upon warnings from significant other as they are observed.

35. Assign patient to develop and process a written after-care plan that addresses specific relapse triggers previously identified.

___. _____

_____

___. _____

_____

___. _____

_____

DIAGNOSTIC SUGGESTIONS

Axis I: 303.90   Alcohol Dependence
             305.00   Alcohol Abuse
             304.30   Cannabis Dependence
             304.20   Cocaine Dependence
             304.80   Polysubstance Dependence
             291.2   Alcohol-Induced Persisting Amnestic Disorder
             300.4   Dysthymic Disorder
             309.81   Posttraumatic Stress Disorder

             _____   _____

Axis II: 301.7   Antisocial Personality Disorder

             _____   _____
             _____   _____

CHILDHOOD TRAUMAS

BEHAVIORAL DEFINITIONS

1. Reports of childhood physical, sexual, or emotional abuse.
2. Description of parents as physically or emotionally neglectful as they were chemically dependent, too busy, absent, and so on.
3. Description of childhood as chaotic as parent(s) was substance abuser (or mentally ill, antisocial, etc.), leading to frequent moves, multiple abusive spousal partners, frequent substitute caretakers, financial pressures, and/or many step-siblings.
4. Reports of emotionally repressive parents who were rigid, perfectionistic, threatening, demeaning, hypercritical, and/or hyperreligious.
5. Irrational fears, suppressed rage, low self-esteem, identity conflicts, depression, or anxious insecurity related to painful early life experiences.
6. Dissociative phenomena (multiple personality, psychogenic fugue or amnesia, trance state, and/or depersonalization) evidenced in behavior as maladaptive coping mechanisms resulting from childhood emotional pain.

—. _____
   _____
—. _____
   _____
—. _____
   _____

LONG-TERM GOALS

1. Develop an awareness of how childhood issues have affected and continue to affect one's family life.
2. Resolve past childhood/family issues, leading to less anger and depression; greater self-esteem, security, and confidence.
3. Release the emotions associated with past childhood/family issues, resulting in less resentment and more serenity.
4. Let go of blame and begin to forgive others for pain caused in childhood.

—. _____
_____
—. _____
_____
—. _____
_____

SHORT-TERM OBJECTIVES

1. Describe what it was like to grow up in the home environment. (1, 2, 3)
2. Describe each family member and how each is perceived and feelings toward each. (2, 3)
3. Identify the role played within the family and feelings associated with that role. (2, 4)
4. Identify feelings associated with major traumatic incidents in childhood. (2, 5, 6, 13)
5. Identify feelings associated with parental child-rearing patterns. (2, 5)

THERAPEUTIC INTERVENTIONS

1. Actively build the level of trust with the patient in individual sessions through consistent eye contact, active listening, unconditional positive regard, and warm acceptance to help increase his/her ability to identify and express feelings.
2. Explore patient's painful childhood experiences.
3. Develop patient's family genogram and/or symptom line and help identify patterns of dysfunction within the family.
4. Assist patient in clarifying his/her role within the family and his/her feelings about that role.

6. Increase awareness of the effects of emotional and behavioral upbringing. (5, 6, 7)

7. Identify how own parenting has been influenced by childhood experiences. (6, 8)

8. Decrease statements of being a victim while increasing statements that reflect personal empowerment. (9, 10, 14)

9. Decrease feelings of shame by being able to verbally affirm self as not responsible for abuse. (7, 11, 12, 13, 14)

10. Increase level of trust of others as shown by more socialization and greater intimacy tolerance. (15, 16)

11. Identify the positive aspects for self of being able to forgive all those involved with the abuse. (17, 18)

12. Verbalize a desire to begin a process of forgiveness for the perpetrator of the pain, for any self-incrimination, and for others who may have been passive collaborators. (13, 17, 18, 19)

13. Identify patterns of abuse, neglect, or abandonment within the family of origin, both current and historical, nuclear and extended. (3, 20)

• 14. State the role substance abuse has in dealing with emotional pain of childhood. (21)

5. Support and encourage patient when he/she begins to express feelings of rage, sadness, fear, and rejection relating to family abuse or neglect.

6. Assign patient to record feelings in a journal that describes memories, behavior, and emotions tied to traumatic childhood experiences.

7. Ask patient to read the books *It Will Never Happen to Me* (Black), *Outgrowing the Pain* (Gil), *Healing the Child Within* (Whitfield), and *Why I'm Afraid to Tell You Who I Am* (Powell), and identify insights attained.

8. Ask patient to compare his/her parenting behavior to that of parent figures of his/her childhood. Encourage patient to be aware of how easily we repeat patterns that we grew up with.

9. Ask patient to complete an exercise that identifies the positives and negatives of being a victim and the positives and negatives of being a survivor. Compare and process list with therapist.

10. Encourage and reinforce statements that reflect movement away from viewing self as a victim and toward personal empowerment as a survivor.

11. Assign writing a letter to mother, father, or whomever in which the patient

15. Acknowledge any dissociative phenomena that have resulted from childhood trauma. (22, 23)

—. _____
    _____

—. _____
    _____

—. _____
    _____

expresses his/her feelings regarding childhood trauma.

12. Hold conjoint session where patient confronts the perpetrator of the abuse.

13. Guide the patient in an empty chair exercise with a key figure connected to the abuse—that is, perpetrator, sibling, or parent.

14. Consistently reiterate that responsibility for the abuse falls on the abusive adults, not the surviving child (for deserving the abuse), and reinforce statements that accurately reflect placing blame on perpetrators and nonprotective, nonnurturent adults.

15. Teach the patient the share-check method of building trust in relationships.

16. Teach patient the advantages of treating people as trustworthy with a reasonable amount of time to assess their character.

17. Teach the benefits to the patient (i.e., release of hurt and anger, putting issue in the past, opens door for trust of others, etc.) of beginning a process of forgiveness of (not necessarily forgetting or fraternizing with) abusive adults.

18. Recommend that patient read *Forgive and Forget* (Smedes) and/or *When Bad Things Happen to Good People* (Kushner).

19. Assign patient to write a forgiveness letter to perpetrator of hurt and process it with therapist.

20. Assign patient to ask parents about their family backgrounds and develop insight regarding patterns of behavior and causes for parents' dysfunction.

21. Assess patient's substance abuse behavior that has developed, in part, as a means of coping with feelings of childhood trauma. If alcohol or drug abuse is found to be a problem, see the "Chemical Dependence" chapter of this *Planner*.

22. Assist patient in understanding the role of dissociation in protecting self from pain of childhood abusive betrayals. (See the "Dissociation" chapter of this *Planner*.)

23. Assess the severity of dissociation phenomena occurring and hospitalize as necessary for patient protection.

__. _____
_____

__. _____
_____

__. _____
_____

DIAGNOSTIC SUGGESTIONS

Axis I:
300.4	Dysthymic Disorder
296.xx	Major Depressive Disorder
300.3	Obsessive-Compulsive Disorder
300.02	Generalized Anxiety Disorder
309.81	Posttraumatic Stress Disorder
300.14	Dissociative Identity Disorder
V61.21	Sexual Abuse of Child (995.5, Victim)
V61.21	Physical Abuse of Child (995.5, Victim)
V61.21	Neglect of Child (995.5, Victim)
_____	_____
_____	_____

Axis II:
301.7	Antisocial Personality Disorder
301.6	Dependent Personality Disorder
301.4	Obsessive-Compulsive Personality Disorder
_____	_____
_____	_____

CHRONIC PAIN

BEHAVIORAL DEFINITIONS

1. Experiences pain beyond the normal healing process (6 months or more) that significantly limits physical activities.
2. Complaints of generalized pain in many joints, muscles, and bones that debilitates normal functioning.
3. Overuse or use of increased amounts of medications with little, if any, pain relief.
4. Experiences tension, migraine, cluster, or chronic daily headaches.
5. Experiences back or neck pain, interstitial cystitis, diabetic neuropathy, or fibromyalgia.
6. Intermittent pain of rheumatoid arthritis or irritable bowel syndrome.
7. Decreased or stopped activities such as work, household chores, socializing, exercise, sex, or other pleasurable activities because of pain.
8. Experiences an increase in physical symptoms (e.g., fatigue, night sweats, insomnia, muscle tension, body aches, decreased concentration, or decreased memory).
9. Exhibits signs and symptoms of depression.
10. Makes statements like "I can't do what I used to"; "No one understands me"; "Why me?"; "When will this go away?"; and "I can't go on."

__. _____
   _____
__. _____
   _____
__. _____
   _____

LONG-TERM GOALS

1. Acquire and utilize the necessary pain management skills.
2. Regulate pain in order to maximize daily functioning and return to productive employment.
3. Find relief from pain and build renewed contentment and joy in performing activities of everyday life.
4. Find an escape route from the pain.
5. "Make peace with his/her chronic pain and move on" (Hunter).
6. Lessen daily suffering from pain.
7. Gain control again over his/her life.

—. _____

_____

—. _____

_____

—. _____

_____

SHORT-TERM OBJECTIVES

1. Describe the nature of, history of, and understood causes for chronic pain. (1)
2. Identify how pain has made an impact on daily activities. (1, 2)
3. Verbalize the mood and attitude changes that have accompanied the experience of chronic pain. (1, 3)
4. Complete a thorough medical examination to rule out any alternative causes for the pain and any new treatment possibilities. (4)
5. Follow through on referral to pain management or rehabilitation program. (5, 6, 7)

THERAPEUTIC INTERVENTIONS

1. Gather a history and current status of the chronic pain.
2. Explore the changes in social, vocational, familial, and intimacy roles that have occurred in accommodation to the pain.
3. Explore the patient's emotional reaction to the chronic pain.
4. Refer patient to a physician or clinic to undergo a thorough examination to rule out any undiagnosed condition and to receive recommendations on any further treatment options.

6. Make a verbal commitment to successfully complete a program for pain or headache management. (8)

7. Complete a thorough medication review by a physician who is specialized in dealing with chronic pain or headache conditions. (9, 10)

8. Verbalize a statement of ownership of the pain. (11, 12)

9. Verbalize an increased understanding of pain. (13, 14)

10. Identify specific non-headache pain triggers. (15, 16, 17)

11. Identify causes for and triggers of headache pain. (16, 17, 18)

12. Identify the steps of the "dance of pain" in his/her life. (16, 17, 19, 20)

13. Increase awareness of the mind-body connection. (14, 21, 22, 23)

14. Attend an educational group or class to learn more about the connection between physical and emotional or mental stress. (23)

15. Implement the use of relaxation techniques to reduce muscle tension and pain level. (24, 25, 26)

16. Utilize yoga and/or meditation to reduce tension and pain. (27, 28)

17. Incorporate physical exercise into daily routine. (29, 30, 31)

5. Give patient information on the options of pain management specialists or rehabilitation programs that are available and help him/her make a decision on which would be the best for him/her.

6. Make referral to pain management specialist or rehabilitation program of patient's choice.

7. Ask patient to sign appropriate releases for therapist to have regular updates on progress from program staff and/or to coordinate services.

8. Elicit from patient a verbal commitment to cooperate with pain management specialist, headache clinic, or rehabilitation program.

9. Ask patient to follow through with a medication review by a physician who specializes in chronic pain or headaches. Then make appropriate referral.

10. Confer with physician regarding recommendations concerning medications after the evaluation.

11. Assist patient in working through the defenses that prevent him/her from owning the pain as his/hers.

12. Elicit from the patient statements of ownership of the pain.

18. Identify dysfunctional attitudes about pain that are a foundation for pain being the focus of life. (32, 33, 34)

19. Verbalize new attitudes about pain that are healthier. (32, 35)

20. Implement the conscious use of humor to keep spirits up and promote healing. (36)

21. Explore the use of alternative pain remedies (e.g., hypnosis, acupuncture, or myotherapy) to reduce dependence on doctor visits and/or painkilling medication. (37)

22. Make changes in diet that will promote health and fitness. (38, 39)

23. Increase the frequency of identified pleasurable activities. (40)

24. Increase the frequency of assertive behaviors in becoming more active in managing his/her life. (41)

25. Identify negative self-talk that promotes helplessness, anger, and depression. (42, 43)

26. Verbalize positive self-talk that promotes empowerment, self-acceptance, and joy. (42, 44, 45)

27. Identify negative "tapes" and those new positive "tapes" that must replace them. (46)

28. Identify sources of stress in daily life. (47, 48)

13. Teach patient key concepts of rehabilitation versus biological healing, conservative versus aggressive medical interventions, acute versus chronic pain, benign versus nonbenign pain, cure versus management, appropriate use of medication, role of exercise and self-regulation techniques, and so on.

14. Assign patient to read *Pain* (Fields), *The Culture of Pain* (Morris), or similar books and to process key concept/insights gained from the reading with therapist.

15. Ask patient to read chapter on "Identifying Pain Triggers" from *Making Peace With Chronic Pain* (Hunter), then make a list of the triggers that apply to his/her condition, and process list with therapist.

16. Ask patient to keep a pain journal which records time of day, where and what he/she was doing, severity, and what was done to alleviate the pain.

17. Process pain journal with patient to increase insight into triggers for and nature of the pain and what interventions may help to alleviate the frequency, duration, and severity of the pain.

18. Assign reading the chapter on "Causes and Triggers" in *Taking Control of Your Headaches* (Duckro,

29. Verbalize the stress-coping steps that will be taken to reduce the impact of stress or physical health. (49)

30. Develop a thorough, realistic relapse prevention plan. (50, 51, 52)

—. _____
   _____

—. _____
   _____

—. _____
   _____

Richardson, and Marshall) or similar information obtained from the National Headache Foundation (800-255-2243).

19. Develop with patient the metaphor of pain as a dance (see *Making Peace With Chronic Pain* by Hunter) then work to identify the particular steps of the dance as it moves through his/her daily life.

20. Challenge patient to either alter the steps of his/her present dance or to design a completely new dance.

21. Ask patient to read *Peace, Love and Healing* (Siegel), *The Mind/Body Effect* (Benson), or similar work for insight into the body-mind connection.

22. Assist patient in beginning to see the connection between chronic pain and chronic stress.

23. Encourage patient to attend a class or seminar related to holistic healing.

24. Teach patient relaxation techniques (e.g., breathing exercises, using a focus word or phrase, progressive muscle relaxation, creating a safe place, and positive imagery).

25. Encourage patient to use relaxation tapes, videos, and so on on a daily basis. Especially recommend "Pachelbel's Canon" by D. Kobialka.

26. Refer for or conduct biofeed-back training with patient to increase relaxation skills.

27. Ask patient to read *How To Meditate* (LeShan) and then assist him/her in implementing mediation into daily life.

28. Refer to beginners' yoga class.

29. Assist patient in recognizing his/her need for regular exercise.

30. Refer patient to an athletic club or a physical therapist to develop an individually tailored exercise program that is approved by patient's personal physician.

31. Encourage patient to implement exercise into daily life and monitor results and offer ongoing encouragement to stay with the regime.

32. Assign Chapter 6 ("The Power of the Mind") and Chapter 7 ("Adopting Healthy Attitudes") from the book *Managing Pain before It Manages You* (Caudill). Process key concepts gathered from reading.

33. Assign patient to complete Dysfunctional Attitude Scale (DAS) in *Managing Pain before It Manages You* (Caudill) and to process results with therapist.

34. Ask patient to gather from several friends, relatives, and so on feedback in terms

of negative attitudes they see in patient. Process feedback and identify possible changes.

35. Confront patient's negative attitudes about pain and assist in replacing them with more positive, constructive attitudes.

36. Assist patient in becoming capable of seeing humor in more of his/her daily life. Promote this expansion with use of humorous teaching tapes, Dr. Seuss, telling jokes, and assigning patient to watch one or two comedy movies each week.

37. Explore alternatives to doctors and medications such as acupuncture, hypnosis or myotherapy (therapeutic) massage.

38. Refer to dietician for consultation around eating and nutritional patterns.

39. Process result of dietician's consultation and identify changes that patient can make and how he/she might start implementing these changes.

40. Ask patient to create a list of activities that are pleasurable to him/her. Then process list with therapist and develop a plan of increasing the frequency of the selected pleasurable activities.

41. Train in assertiveness or refer patient to a group that will educate and facilitate assertiveness skills via lectures and assignments.

42. Assign the chapter in *The Feeling Good Handbook* (Burns) entitled "You Can Change the Way You Feel" where 10 cognitive distortions are defined.

43. Assist patient in identifying his/her distorted automatic thoughts that promote depression, helplessness, and/or anger.

44. Assign patient to complete the written exercises in Step 2: "You *Feel* the Way You Think" from *Ten Days to Self Esteem!* (Burns). Process exercises when completed.

45. Assist patient in replacing negative, distorted thoughts with positive, reality-based thoughts.

46. Utilize a Transactional Analysis (TA) approach to help patient become aware of "old tapes," and using same approach, begin to erase them or create new healthier "tapes."

47. Ask patient to list the stressors he/she feels in daily life and process list with therapist.

48. Educate patient on the many types of internal, external, and family stressors to help increase overall stress awareness.

49. Assist patient in identifying specific ways to cope effectively with the major internal, external, and family stressors.

50. Assist patient in developing a written relapse prevention plan that has a special emphasis on pain- and stress-trigger identification and specific ways to handle each.

51. Review and probe relapse prevention plan with patient and redirect or firm up areas that are weak or lack an adequate level of thought or planning.

52. Assign patient to share relapse prevention plan with those who are going to be part of his/her support system so they might help with implementation, support, and feedback of the plan.

__. _____
   _____

__. _____
   _____

__. _____
   _____

DIAGNOSTIC SUGGESTIONS

Axis I:	307.89	Pain Disorder Associated with Both Psychological Factors and an Axis III Disorder
	307.80	Pain Disorder Associated with Psychological Factors
	300.81	Somatization Disorder
	300.11	Conversion Disorder
	296.3	Major Depressive Disorder, Recurrent
	300.3	Obsessive-Compulsive Disorder
	302.70	Sexual Dysfunction NOS
	304.10	Sedative, Hypnotic, or Anxiolytic Dependence
	304.80	Polysubstance Dependence
	_____	_____
	_____	_____

COGNITIVE DEFICITS

BEHAVIORAL DEFINITIONS

1. Concrete thinking or impaired abstract thinking.
2. Lack of insight into the consequences of behavior or impaired judgment.
3. Short-term or long-term memory deficits.
4. Difficulty following complex or sequential directions.
5. Loss of orientation to time, person, or place.
6. Distractibility in attention.
7. Impulsive behavior that violates social mores.
8. Speech and language impairment.

—. _____
   _____
   _____
—. _____
   _____
   _____
—. _____
   _____

LONG-TERM GOALS

1. Determine the degree and cause of cognitive impairment.
2. Develop alternative coping strategies to compensate for cognitive limitations.

—. _____
   _____

—. _____
_____
—. _____
_____

SHORT-TERM OBJECTIVES

1. Describe all symptoms that may be related to neurological deficit. (1, 2)
2. Cooperate with and complete neuropsychological testing. (3, 4)
3. Obtain a neurological examination. (5)
4. Understand and accept cognitive limitations and use alternate coping mechanisms. (6, 7)
5. Verbalize feelings associated with acceptance of cognitive impairment. (8)
6. Demonstrate the ability to follow through to completion of simple sequential tasks. (9)
7. Implement memory-enhancing mechanisms. (9, 10)
8. Identify when it is appropriate to seek help with a task and when it is not. (6, 11)
9. State a preference for who will be a resource person to provide guidance and supervision when necessary. (12)
10. Write a plan for when and who will provide daily supervisory contact. (13)

THERAPEUTIC INTERVENTIONS

1. Explore signs and symptoms of possible neurological impairment (e.g., memory, coordination, abstract thinking, speech and language, executive functions, orientation, impaired judgment, attention, headaches, dizziness, blurry vision, etc.).
2. Assess and monitor cognitive behavior in individual sessions.
3. Arrange for patient to have psychological testing to determine nature and degree of cognitive deficits.
4. Administer appropriate psychological tests (e.g., Wechsler Adult Intelligence Scale—III, Booklet Category Test, Trailmaking, Halstead-Reitan Battery, Michigan Neurological Battery, Luria-Nebraska Battery, Wechsler Memory Scale, and Memory Assessment Scales) to determine nature, extent, and possible origin of cognitive deficits.

—. _____
    _____
—. _____
    _____
—. _____
    _____

5. Refer to neurologist, if appropriate, to further assess organic deficits and possible causes.

6. Discuss results of testing with psychologist and develop appropriate objectives based on testing.

7. Assist patient in coming to an understanding and acceptance of limitations.

8. Explore feelings of depression and anxiety related to cognitive impairment. Provide encouragement and support.

9. Assign appropriate sequential tasks for patient to follow through on and redirect when needed so as to assess cognitive abilities.

10. Assign and monitor memory-enhancing activities/ exercises (e.g., crossword puzzles, card games, or TV game shows) and memory-loss coping strategies (e.g., lists, routines, labeling, etc.)

11. Establish with patient and significant other appropriate points for patient to ask for help.

12. Assist patient in identifying acceptable resource people who can provide regular supervision.

13. Develop a written plan with patient for persons and times of supervisory contact.

—. _____
    _____
—. _____
    _____
—. _____
    _____

DIAGNOSTIC SUGGESTIONS

Axis I:

	310.1	Personality Change Due to (Axis III Disorder)
	294.8	Dementia NOS
	294.1	Dementia Due to (Axis III Disorder)
	291.2	Alcohol-Induced Persisting Dementia
	291.1	Alcohol-Induced Persisting Amnestic Disorder
	294.8	Amnestic Disorder NOS
	303.90	Alcohol Dependence
	304.30	Cannabis Dependence
	294.0	Amnestic Disorder Due to (Axis III Disorder)
	294.9	Cognitive Disorder NOS

_____ _____

_____ _____

DEPENDENCY

BEHAVIORAL DEFINITIONS

1. Inability to become self-sufficient, consistently relying on parents to provide financial support, housing, or caregiving.
2. A history of many intimate relationships with little, if any, space between the ending of one and the start of the next.
3. Strong feelings of panic, fear, and helplessness when faced with being alone as a close relationship ends.
4. Feels easily hurt by criticism and is preoccupied with pleasing others.
5. Inability to make decisions or initiate action without excessive re-assurance from others.
6. Frequent preoccupation with fears of being abandoned.
7. All feelings of self-worth, happiness, and fulfillment derive from relationships.
8. Involvement in at least two relationships in which he/she was physically abused but had difficulty leaving.
9. Avoids disagreement with others for fear of being rejected.

__. _____
    _____
__. _____
    _____
__. _____
    _____

LONG-TERM GOALS

1. Develop confidence in self that he/she is capable of meeting his/her own needs and of tolerating being alone.
2. Achieve a balance between healthy independence and healthy dependence.
3. Decrease dependence on relationships while beginning to meet his/her own needs, build confidence, and practice assertiveness.
4. Establish firm individual self-boundaries and improved self-worth.
5. Break away permanently from an abusive relationship.
6. Emancipate self from emotional and economic dependence on parents.

—. _____
   _____
—. _____
   _____
—. _____
   _____

SHORT-TERM OBJECTIVES	THERAPEUTIC INTERVENTIONS
1. Describe the style and pattern of emotional dependence in relationships. (1)	1. Explore patient's history of emotional dependence beginning with unmet needs in family of origin to current relationships.
2. Verbalize an increased awareness of his/her dependency. (2, 3)	2. Assign patient to read *Codependent No More* (Beattie), *Women Who Love Too Much* (Norwood), or *Getting Them Sober* (Drews). Process key ideas.
3. Verbalize insight into the automatic practice of striving to meet other people's expectations. (2, 4, 5, 6)	
4. Identify and clarify own emotional and social needs. (7)	3. Develop a family genogram to increase patient's awareness of family patterns of dependence in relationships and how he/she is repeating them in the present relationship.
5. Increase attempts to fulfill own needs. (2, 7, 8, 11)	

6. Report incidents of verbally stating his/her opinion. (9, 10, 11)

7. Increase saying no to others' requests. (5, 13)

8. Verbalize a decreased sensitivity to criticism. (4, 5, 12, 13, 14)

9. Report examples of allowing others to do things for him/her and to receive without giving. (2, 15)

10. Verbalize an increased sense of self-responsibility while decreasing sense of responsibility for others. (16, 17, 18, 20, 21)

11. Verbalize an increased awareness of boundaries and when they are violated. (17, 19, 21)

12. Increase the frequency of verbally clarifying boundaries with others. (9, 11, 20, 21, 22)

13. Increase the frequency of making decisions within a reasonable time and with self-assurance. (4, 5, 10, 11, 23)

14. List positive things about self. (24, 25)

15. Identify distorted automatic thoughts associated with assertiveness, being alone, or keeping personal responsibility boundaries. (26, 27)

16. Verbalize positive, reality-based self-talk that must replace distorted cognitive messages. (24, 28)

4. Explore family of origin for experiences of emotional abandonment.

5. Assist patient in identifying the basis for the fear of disappointing others.

6. Read with patient the fable entitled "The Bridge" in *Friedman's Fables* (Friedman). Process the meaning of the fable.

7. Ask patient to put together a list of emotional and social needs and ways that these could possibly be met. Process list.

8. Ask patient to list ways he/she could start taking care of himself/herself; then identify two to three that could be started now and elicit patient's agreement to do so. Monitor for follow-through and feelings of change about self.

9. Assign patient to speak his/her mind for one day and to process the results with therapist.

10. Train in assertiveness or refer patient to a group that will educate and facilitate assertiveness skills via lectures and assignments.

11. Verbally reinforce any and all signs of assertiveness and independence.

12. Assign patient to say no without excessive explanation for a period of one week and process this with therapist.

17. Attend an Alanon group to reinforce attempts to break dependency cycle with an alcoholic partner. (29)

18. Develop a plan to end relationship with abusive partner and implement the plan with therapist's guidance. (30, 31, 32)

—. _____

_____

—. _____

_____

—. _____

_____

13. Assign patient to read *When I Say No I Feel Guilty* (Smith).

14. Explore patient's sensitivity to criticism and help develop new ways of receiving, processing and responding to it.

15. Assign patient to allow others to do for him/her and to receive without giving. Process progress and feelings related to this assignment.

16. Assist patient in identifying and implementing ways of increasing his/her level of independence in day-to-day life.

17. Assist patient in developing new boundaries for not accepting responsibility for others' actions or feelings.

18. Facilitate conjoint session with patient's significant other with focus on exploring ways to increase independence within the relationship.

19. Assign patient to journal daily regarding boundaries for taking responsibility for self and others and when he/she is aware of boundaries being broken by self or others.

20. Assign patient to read the book *Boundaries: Where You End and I Begin* (Katherine) and process key ideas with therapist.

21. Ask patient to read the chapter on setting boundaries and limits in the book *A Gift To Myself* (Whitfield) and complete survey on personal boundaries that is part of the chapter. Process key ideas and results of survey with therapist.

22. Reinforce patient for implementing boundaries and limits for self.

23. Confront patient's decision avoidance and encourage decision-making process.

24. Assist patient in developing a list of positive attributes and accomplishments.

25. Assign patient to institute a ritual of beginning each day with 5 to 10 minutes of solitude where the focus is personal affirmation.

26. Explore and identify patient's distorted, negative automatic thoughts associated with assertiveness, being alone, or not meeting other's needs.

27. Explore and clarify fears of other feelings associated with being more independent.

28. Assist patient in developing positive, reality-based messages for self that must replace the distorted, negative self-talk.

29. Refer to Alanon or another appropriate self-help group.

30. Assign patient to read *The Verbally Abusive Relationship* (Evans) and process key ideas and insights gathered from reading with therapist.

31. Refer to a safe house.

32. Refer to a specific domestic violence program and monitor and encourage patient's continued involvement in the program.

___. _____
_____

___. _____
_____

___. _____
_____

DIAGNOSTIC SUGGESTIONS

Axis I:	300.4	Dysthymic Disorder
	V61.1	Physical Abuse of Adult (995.81, Victim)
	___	_____
	___	_____
Axis II:	301.82	Avoidant Personality Disorder
	301.83	Borderline Personality Disorder
	301.6	Dependent Personality Disorder
	___	_____
	___	_____

DEPRESSION

BEHAVIORAL DEFINITIONS

1. Loss of appetite.
2. Depressed affect.
3. Diminished interest in or enjoyment of activities.
4. Psychomotor agitation or retardation.
5. Sleeplessness or hypersomnia.
6. Lack of energy.
7. Poor concentration and indecisiveness.
8. Social withdrawal.
9. Suicidal thoughts and/or gestures.
10. Feelings of hopelessness, worthlessness, or inappropriate guilt.
11. Low self-esteem.
12. Unresolved grief issues.
13. Mood-related hallucinations or delusions.
14. History of chronic or recurrent depression for which client has taken antidepressant medication, been hospitalized, had outpatient treatment, or had a course of electroconvulsive therapy.

__. _____
  _____

__. _____
  _____

__. _____
  _____

LONG-TERM GOALS

1. Alleviate depressed mood and return to previous level of effective functioning.

2. Develop the ability to recognize, accept, and cope with feelings of depression.
3. Develop healthy cognitive patterns and beliefs about self and the world that lead to alleviation of depression symptoms.
4. Appropriately grieve the loss in order to normalize mood and to return to previous adaptive level of functioning.

—. _____

  _____

—. _____

  _____

—. _____

  _____

SHORT-TERM OBJECTIVES

1. Describe the signs and symptoms of depression that are experienced. (1, 3)

2. Verbally identify, if possible, the source of depressed mood. (2, 3)

3. Begin to experience sadness in session while discussing the disappointment related to the loss or pain from the past. (3, 4)

4. Express feelings of hurt, disappointment, shame, and anger that are associated with early life experiences. (3, 4, 5, 6)

5. Verbally express understanding of the relationship between depressed mood and repression of feelings— that is, anger, hurt, sadness, and so on. (5, 6)

THERAPEUTIC INTERVENTIONS

1. Explore how depression is experienced in patient's day-to-day living.

2. Ask patient to make a list of what he/she is depressed about and process list with therapist.

3. Encourage sharing feelings of depression in order to clarify them and gain insight as to causes.

4. Explore experiences from the patient's childhood that contribute to current depressed state.

5. Encourage patient to share feelings of anger regarding pain inflicted on him/her in childhood that contributes to current depressed state.

6. Explain a connection between previously unex-

6. Take prescribed medications responsibly at times ordered by physician. (7, 8)

7. Report to appropriate professional the effectiveness of medications and any side effects. (8)

8. Complete psychological testing to assess the depth of depression and the need for antidepressant medication and suicide prevention measures. (9)

9. Verbalize any history of suicide attempts and any current suicidal urges. (9, 10)

10. Identify cognitive self-talk that is engaged in to support depression. (11)

11. Keep a daily record of dysfunctional thinking that includes each situation associated with depressed feelings and the thoughts that triggered those feelings. (11, 12, 30)

12. Replace negative and self-defeating self-talk with verbalization of realistic and positive cognitive messages. (12, 13, 30)

13. State no longer having thoughts of self-harm. (14, 15)

14. Show evidence of daily care for personal grooming and hygiene with minimal reminders from others. (16)

15. Make positive statements regarding self and ability to cope with stresses of life. (13, 17)

pressed (repressed) feelings of anger (and helplessness) and current state of depression.

7. Arrange for physician to give a physical examination to rule out organic causes for depression, assess need for antidepressant medication, and arrange for a prescription, if appropriate.

8. Monitor and evaluate medication compliance and the effectiveness of the medications on level of functioning.

9. Arrange for administration of Beck Depression Inventory, Minnesota Multiphasic Personality Inventory-2, Modified Scale for Suicidal Ideation, or other objective assessment instrument. Evaluate results and give feedback to patient.

10. Explore history and current state of suicidal urges and behavior. (See interventions designed for Suicidal Ideation in this *Planner* if suicide risk is present).

11. Assist in developing awareness of cognitive messages that reinforce hopelessness and helplessness.

12. Help the patient keep a daily record that lists each situation associated with the depressed feelings and the dysfunctional thinking that triggered the depression. Then use logic and reality to challenge each dysfunctional thought for

16. Verbalize hopeful and positive statements regarding the future. (13, 17, 18)

17. Utilize behavioral strategies to overcome depression. (19, 20, 21)

18. Engage in physical and recreational activities that reflect increased energy and interest. (19, 21)

19. Participate in social contacts and initiate communication of needs and desires. (19, 22)

20. Verbalize any unresolved grief issues that may be contributing to depression. (23)

21. Read books on overcoming depression. (24)

22. Use positive conflict resolution skills to resolve interpersonal discord and to make needs and expectations known. (25, 26)

23. Increase frequency of assertive behaviors to express needs, desires, and expectations. (22, 27)

24. Decrease frequency of negative self-descriptive statements and increase frequency of positive self-descriptive statements. (17, 28, 29)

25. Keep a daily journal of experiences, thoughts, and feelings to clarify instances of distorted negative thinking or perception that pre-

accuracy, replacing it with a positive, accurate thought.

13. Reinforce positive, reality-based cognitive messages that enhance self-confidence and increase adaptive action.

14. Assess and monitor suicide potential.

15. Arrange for hospitalization, as necessary, when patient is judged to be harmful to self.

16. Monitor and redirect patient on daily grooming and hygiene.

17. Assign patient to write at least one positive affirmation statement daily regarding himself/herself and the future.

18. Assist in teaching more about depression and accepting some sadness as a normal variation in feeling.

19. Assist patient in developing coping strategies (e.g., more physical exercise, less internal focus, increased social involvement, more assertiveness, greater need sharing, more anger expression, etc.) for feelings of depression.

20. Assign chemically dependent patient to read passages related to depression from the books *One Day at a Time* (Hallinan) and *Each Day a New Beginning* (Hazelden Staff).

21. Develop a plan for participation in recreational activities.

cipitate depressive emotions. (30)

26. Implement a regular exercise regimen as a depression reduction technique. (31, 32)

—. _____
_____

—. _____
_____

—. _____
_____

22. Reinforce social activities and verbalization of feelings, needs, and desires.

23. Explore the role of unresolved grief issues as they contribute to current depression. (See Interventions suggested for Grief/Loss Unresolved in this *Planner* if applicable).

24. Recommend self-help books on coping with depression (e.g., *The Feeling Good Handbook* by Burns, *What to Say When You Talk to Yourself* by Helmstetter, or *Talking to Yourself* by Butler).

25. Teach the patient conflict resolution skills (e.g., empathy, active listening, "I messages," respectful communication, assertiveness without aggression, compromise); then use modeling, role-playing, and behavior rehearsal to work through several current conflicts.

26. In conjoint sessions, help the patient resolve interpersonal conflicts and problems.

27. Use modeling and/or role-playing to train in assertiveness. If indicated refer to an assertiveness training class/group for further instruction.

28. Assign exercise of patient talking positively about self into a mirror once per day.

29. Reinforce patient's positive statements made about self.

30. Assign patient to keep a daily journal of experiences, automatic negative thoughts associated with experiences, and the depressive affect that results from that distorted interpretation. Process journal material to diffuse destructive thinking patterns and replace with alternate, realistic, positive thoughts.

31. Develop and reinforce a routine of physical exercise to stimulate depression-reducing hormones.

32. Recommend that the patient read and implement programs from *Exercising Your Way to Better Mental Health* (Leith).

—. _____
_____

—. _____
_____

—. _____
_____

DIAGNOSTIC SUGGESTIONS

Axis I:		
	309.0	Adjustment Disorder with Depressed Mood
	296.xx	Bipolar I Disorder
	296.89	Bipolar II Disorder
	300.4	Dysthymic Disorder
	301.13	Cyclothymic Disorder
	296.2x	Major Depressive Disorder, Single Episode
	296.3x	Major Depressive Disorder, Recurrent
	295.70	Schizoaffective Disorder
	310.1	Personality Change Due to (Axis III Disorder)
	V62.82	Bereavement
	_____	_____
	_____	_____

DISSOCIATION

BEHAVIORAL DEFINITIONS

1. The existence of two or more distinct personalities or personality-states that recurrently take full control of one's behavior.
2. An episode of sudden inability to remember important personal information that is more than just ordinary forgetfulness.
3. Persistent or recurrent experiences of depersonalization, feeling as if detached from or outside of one's mental processes or body during which reality testing remains intact.
4. Persistent or recurrent experiences of depersonalization, feeling as if one is automated or in a dream.
5. Depersonalization sufficiently severe and persistent as to cause marked distress in daily life.

__. _____
   _____
__. _____
   _____
__. _____
   _____

LONG-TERM GOALS

1. Begin the process of integrating the various personalities.
2. Reduce the frequency and duration of dissociative episodes.
3. Resolve the emotional trauma that underlies the dissociative disturbance.
4. Reduce the level of daily distress caused by dissociative disturbances.

5. Regain full memory.

___. _____

_____

___. _____

_____

___. _____

_____

SHORT-TERM OBJECTIVES

1. Identify each personality and have each tell its story. (1, 2)

2. Complete a medication evaluation with a physician. (3)

3. Take prescribed medications responsibly at times ordered by physician. (4)

4. Identify key issues that trigger dissociative state. (5, 6)

5. Decrease number and duration of personality changes. (7, 8)

6. Practice relaxation and deep breathing as means of reducing anxiety. (9)

7. Verbalize acceptance of brief episodes of dissociation as not being the basis for panic but only as passing phenomena. (10)

8. Discuss period preceding memory loss and period after memory returns. (5, 11, 12)

THERAPEUTIC INTERVENTIONS

1. Actively build the level of trust with the patient in individual sessions through consistent eye contact, active listening, unconditional positive regard, and warm acceptance to help increase his/her ability to identify and express feelings.

2. Probe and assess, without undue encouragement or leading, the existence of the various personalities that take control of the patient.

3. Arrange for an evaluation for medications.

4. Monitor and evaluate patient's medication compliance and the effectiveness of the medication on the level of functioning.

5. Explore sources of emotional pain, feelings of fear, inadequacy, rejection, or abuse.

9. Attend family therapy sessions that focus on the recall of personal history information. (11, 13)

10. Cooperate with a referral to a neurologist to rule out organic factors in amnestic episodes. (12)

11. Utilize photos and other memorabilia to stimulate recall of personal history. (13, 14)

—. _____
   _____
—. _____
   _____
—. _____
   _____

6. Assist patient in acceptance of connection between dissociating and avoidance of facing emotional conflicts/issues.

7. Facilitate integration of personality by supporting and encouraging patient to stay focused on reality rather than escape through dissociating.

8. Emphasize the importance of and reinforce instances of a here-and-now focus on reality rather than a preoccupation with the traumas of the past and dissociative phenomena associated with that fixation.

9. Train patient in relaxation and deep breathing techniques to be used for anxiety management.

10. Teach patient to be calm and matter-of-fact in the face of brief dissociative phenomena so as to not accelerate anxiety symptoms but to stay focused on reality.

11. Arrange and facilitate a session with significant others and patient to assist in regaining lost personal information.

12. Refer patient to a neurologist for evaluation of any organic cause for memory loss experiences.

13. Reassure patient calmly to be patient in seeking to regain lost memories.

14. Utilize pictures and other
     memorabilia to gently trig-
     ger memory recall.

___. _____

      _____

___. _____

      _____

___. _____

      _____

DIAGNOSTIC SUGGESTIONS

Axis I: 303.90   Alcohol Dependence
              300.14   Dissociative Identity Disorder
              300.12   Dissociative Amnesia
              300.6   Depersonalization Disorder
              300.15   Dissociative Disorder NOS

_____   _____

_____   _____

EATING DISORDER

BEHAVIORAL DEFINITIONS

1. Chronic, rapid consumption of large quantities of high-carbohydrate food.
2. Self-induced vomiting and/or abuse of laxatives due to fear of weight gain.
3. Extreme weight loss (and amenorrhea in females) with refusal to maintain a minimal healthy weight.
4. Very limited ingestion of food and high frequency of secret self-induced vomiting, inappropriate use of laxatives, and/or excessive strenuous exercise.
5. Persistent preoccupation with body image related to grossly inaccurate assessment of self as overweight.
6. Predominating irrational fear of becoming overweight.
7. Escalating fluid and electrolyte imbalance resulting from eating disorder.
8. Strong denial of seeing self as emaciated even when severely under recommended weight.

___. _____

_____

___. _____

_____

___. _____

_____

LONG-TERM GOALS

1. Restore normal eating patterns, body weight, balanced fluid and electrolytes, and a realistic perception of body size.

2. Terminate the pattern of binge eating and purging behavior with a return to normal eating of enough nutritious foods to maintain a healthy weight.
3. Stabilize the medical conditions, resume patterns of food intake that will sustain life, and gain weight to a normal level.
4. Gain sufficient insight into the cognitive and emotional struggle to allow termination of the eating disorder and responsible maintenance of nutritional food intake.
5. Develop alternate coping strategies (i.e., feeling identification and assertiveness) to deal with underlying emotional issues, making the eating disorder unnecessary.
6. Gain awareness of the interconnectedness of low self-esteem and society pressures with dieting, binge eating, and purging, in order to eliminate eating-disorder behaviors.
7. Change the definition of the self, so that it does not focus on weight, size, and shape as the primary criteria for self-acceptance.
8. Restructure the distorted thoughts, beliefs, and values that contribute to eating-disorder development.

—. _____
   _____
   _____
—. _____
   _____
   _____
—. _____
   _____

SHORT-TERM OBJECTIVES

1. Honestly describe pattern of eating as to frequency, amounts, and types of food consumed or hoarded. (1, 2, 6)

2. Disclose any habit of self-induced vomiting to control caloric intake. (3, 6)

3. Describe any regular use of laxatives to reduce body weight. (4, 6)

THERAPEUTIC INTERVENTIONS

1. Document the reality of a dysfunctional eating pattern (too little food, too much food and/or binge eating, or hoarding food).

2. Compare patient's calorie consumption with an average adult rate of 1,500 calories per day to establish the reality of over- or undereating.

4. Acknowledge frequent use of vigorous exercise to control weight gain. (5, 6)

5. Admit to a persistent preoccupation with body image/size. (7)

6. Cooperate with a complete physical exam. (8, 9)

7. Submit to a dental exam. (10)

8. Cooperate with an evaluation for psychotropic medications. (11, 12)

9. Take medications as ordered and report as to effectiveness and side effects. (12, 13)

10. Comply with psychological testing. (14, 15)

11. Cooperate with admission to inpatient treatment if a fragile medical condition necessitates such treatment. (8, 9, 16)

12. Eat at regular intervals (three meals a day), consuming at least the minimum daily calories necessary to progressively gain weight. (17, 18, 19, 20)

13. Keep a journal of food consumption. (21, 22)

14. Attain and maintain balanced fluids and electrolytes as well as resumption of reproductive functions. (8, 9, 17, 18, 23)

15. Keep a daily journal of thoughts and feelings associated with eating behavior. (24)

3. Explore the existence of vomiting behavior to purge self of calorie intake.

4. Document any abuse of laxatives in an effort to control weight.

5. Explore a history of too vigorous and too frequent exercise in an effort to control weight.

6. Monitor on an ongoing basis patient's vomiting frequency, food hoarding, exercise levels, and laxative usage.

7. Explore patient's perception of body image/size and the frequency and intensity of thinking about it.

8. Refer to physician for physical exam.

9. Stay in close consultation with physician as to patient's medical condition and nutritional habits.

10. Refer to dentist for dental exam.

11. Assess the patient's need for psychotropic medications.

12. Arrange for a physician to evaluate for and then prescribe psychotropic medications.

13. Monitor medication effectiveness and side effects.

14. Arrange for the administration of psychological testing to assess current emotional functioning and aid in differential diagnosis of any coexisting conditions.

16. Identify irrational beliefs and distorted self-talk messages associated with eating normal amounts of food. (24, 25)

17. Verbalize positive, healthy, and rational self-talk associated with eating that will encourage normal food intake. (26, 27)

18. Identify irrational beliefs and expectations regarding body size. (25, 28, 29)

19. Verbalize positive, reality-based self-talk regarding weight status and body size. (20, 26, 27, 28, 29)

20. Verbalize how the fear of sexual identity and development has influenced severe weight loss. (30, 31)

21. Verbalize acceptance of sexual impulses and a desire for intimacy. (30, 31, 32)

22. Identify the relationship between the fear of failure, drive for perfectionism, and the roots of low self-esteem. (33, 34)

23. Verbalize acceptance of shortcomings and normal failures as part of the human condition. (34, 35)

24. Acknowledge and overcome the role that passive-aggressive control (e.g., the refusal to accept guidance) has in the avoidance of eating. (36, 37)

15. Give feedback to the patient (and his/her family) regarding psychological testing results.

16. Refer the patient for hospitalization, as necessary, if his/her weight loss becomes severe and physical health is jeopardized.

17. Establish a minimum daily caloric intake for the patient.

18. Assist the patient in meal planning.

19. Monitor weight and give realistic feedback regarding body thinness.

20. Establish healthy weight goals for the patient per the Body Mass Index (BMI = pounds of body weight × 700/height in inches/height in inches; normal range is 20 to 27 and below 18 is medically critical), the Metropolitan Height and Weight Tables, or some other recognized standard.

21. Assign patient to keep a journal of food intake, thoughts, and feelings.

22. Process journal information.

23. Refer patient back to physician at regular intervals if fluids and electrolytes need monitoring due to poor nutritional habits.

24. Assign the patient to keep a journal of daily thoughts and feelings associated with eating behavior.

25. Acknowledge and resolve separation anxiety related to the emancipation process. (38, 39)

26. Acknowledge to family members the feelings of fear related to separation and state the need for them to reinforce independence. (38, 39, 40)

27. Disclose to family members feelings of ambivalence regarding control and dependency. (33, 36, 38, 40)

28. Develop assertive behaviors that allow for healthy expression of needs and emotions. (40, 41, 42, 43)

29. Verbalize the feelings of low self-esteem, depression, loneliness, anger, need for nurturance, or lack of trust that underlie the eating disorder. (24, 43, 44)

30. State a basis for positive identity that is not based on weight and appearance but on character, traits, relationships, and intrinsic value. (34, 45, 46)

31. Verbalize the connection between suppressed emotional expression, difficulty with interpersonal issues, and unhealthy food usage. (41, 42, 43, 47)

32. Understand and verbalize the connection between too-restrictive dieting and binge episodes. (48, 49)

33. Have significant others state a detachment from re-

25. Assist in the identification of negative cognitive messages (e.g., catastrophizing or exaggerating) that mediate the patient's avoidance of food intake.

26. Train the patient to establish realistic cognitive messages regarding food intake and body size.

27. Reinforce the patient's use of more realistic, positive messages to himself/herself regarding food intake and body size.

28. Confront the patient's unrealistic assessment of his/her body image and assign exercises (e.g., positive self-talk in the mirror, shopping for clothes that flatter the appearance) that reinforce a healthy, realistic body appraisal.

29. Confront the patient's irrational perfectionism in body image expectations and assist in his/her reasonable acceptance of the body with flaws.

30. Process fears regarding sexual development and sexual impulses.

31. Discuss the patient's fear of losing control of sexual impulses and how the fear relates to keeping himself/herself unattractively thin or fat.

32. Reinforce acceptance of sexual impulses and a desire for intimacy as normal.

sponsibility for the patient's eating disorder. (50, 51)

34. Verbalize the acceptance of full responsibility for choices about eating behavior. (52, 53)

35. Gradually accept personal responsibility for adequate nutrition as evidenced by progressive weight gain or maintenance of adequate weight without supervision from others. (53)

36. Terminate inappropriate laxative use. (1, 8, 54)

37. Terminate self-induced vomiting. (5, 8, 55)

38. Stop hoarding food. (1, 8, 56)

39. Set reasonable limits on physical exercise. (5, 8, 57)

40. Gain weight at a rate of two pounds per week (e.g., one pound by Monday and another by Thursday). (19, 20, 58)

41. Meet with dietary specialist to improve dietary habits. (52, 53, 59)

42. Attend an eating disorder group. (60)

__. _____
    _____

__. _____
    _____

__. _____
    _____

33. Discuss the patient's ... failure and the role of perfectionism in the search for control and the avoidance of failure.

34. Reinforce the patient's positive qualities and successes to reduce the fear of failure and build a positive sense of self.

35. Teach and reinforce an acceptance of self and others as human and subject to shortcomings and imperfection. If appropriate, use patient's spiritual belief system to strengthen this concept.

36. Process issue of passive-aggressive control in rebellion against authority figures.

37. Discuss issue of food control as related to fear of losing control of eating or weight.

38. Discuss fears related to independence and emancipation from parent figures.

39. Hold family therapy sessions that focus on issues of separation, dependency, and emancipation.

40. Support and encourage patient in identifying fears related to separation and in making a declaration of independence.

41. Train in assertiveness or refer to an assertiveness training class.

42. Reinforce assertiveness behaviors in session and reports of successful assertiveness between sessions.

43. Facilitate family therapy sessions that focus on owning feelings, clarifying messages, identifying control conflicts, and developing age-appropriate boundaries.

44. Probe the patient's emotional struggles that are camouflaged by the eating disorder.

45. Assist the patient in identifying a basis for self-worth apart from body image by reviewing his/her talents, successes, positive traits, importance to others, and intrinsic spiritual value.

46. Assign the patient the book *Body Traps* (Rodin) and process the key ideas regarding obsessing over body image.

47. Teach the connection between suppressed emotions, interpersonal conflict, and dysfunctional eating behavior.

48. Assist the patient in understanding the relationship between binging and lack of regular mealtimes or total deprivation from specific foods.

49. Encourage the patient to read book(s) on binge eating (e.g., *Overcoming Binge*

Eating by Fairburn) to increase the awareness of the components of eating disorders.

50. Teach parents or partner how to successfully detach from taking responsibility for the patient's eating behavior without becoming hostile or indifferent.

51. Recommend that the patient's parents, partner, or friends read *Surviving an Eating Disorder* (Siegel, et al.) and process the concepts in a family therapy session.

52. Refer the patient to a dietician for education in healthy eating and nutritional concerns.

53. Reinforce weight gain and acceptance of personal responsibility for normal food intake.

54. Set goal of no inappropriate use of laxatives.

55. Set goal of termination of all self-induced vomiting.

56. Set goal of termination of food hoarding.

57. Set goal of very limited or no vigorous exercise.

58. Set goal of a weight gain of two pounds per week.

59. Process meeting with nutritionist as to concrete plans for meal planning and caloric consumption.

60. Refer to support group for eating disorders.

—. _____
   _____
   _____
—. _____
   _____
   _____
—. _____
   _____
   _____

DIAGNOSTIC SUGGESTIONS

Axis I: 307.1   Anorexia Nervosa
              307.51   Bulimia Nervosa
              307.50   Eating Disorder NOS

              _____   _____

              _____   _____

Axis II: 301.6   Dependent Personality Disorder

              _____   _____

              _____   _____

EDUCATIONAL DEFICITS

BEHAVIORAL DEFINITIONS

1. Incompletion of requirements for high school diploma or GED.
2. Possession of no marketable employment skills and need for vocational training.
3. Functional illiteracy.
4. History of difficulties, not involving behavior, in school or other academic or learning situations.

__. _____
   _____

__. _____
   _____

__. _____
   _____

LONG-TERM GOALS

1. Recognize the need for high school completion or GED and reenroll in the necessary courses.
2. Seek out vocational training to obtain marketable employment skill.
3. Increase literacy skills.
4. Receive a high school diploma or GED certificate.
5. Establish the existence of a learning disability and begin the development of skills to overcome it.

—. _____
   _____
   _____
—. _____
   _____
   _____
—. _____
   _____

SHORT-TERM OBJECTIVES

1. Identify the factors that contributed to termination of education. (1, 6)

2. Identify the negative consequences that have occurred due to lack of high school completion. (2, 3)

3. Verbally verify the need for a high school diploma or GED. (4, 5)

4. Describe personal and family educational achievements and struggles. (6)

5. Complete an assessment to identify style of learning and to establish or rule out a specific learning disability. (7)

6. Cooperate with a psychological assessment for symptoms of Attention Deficit Disorder (ADD) that may have interfered with educational achievement. (8, 9)

7. Take medication as prescribed, reporting as to effectiveness and side effects. (9, 10)

THERAPEUTIC INTERVENTIONS

1. Explore patient's attitude toward education and the family, peer, and/or school experiences that led to termination of education.

2. Confront patient with the need for further education.

3. Assist patient in listing the negative effects that the lack of a GED or high school diploma has had on his/her life.

4. Support and direct patient toward obtaining further academic training.

5. Reinforce and encourage patient in pursuing educational and/or vocational training by pointing out the social, monetary, and self-esteem advantages.

6. Gather an educational history from patient that includes family achievement history and difficulties patient had in regard to specific subjects (e.g., reading, math, etc.).

8. Implement the recommendations of evaluations. (11)

9. Verbalize decreased anxiety and negativity associated with learning situations. (12, 13)

10. Identify the negative, critical education-related experiences endured from parents, teachers, or peers. (14, 15)

11. Verbalize feelings of shame or embarrassment associated with academic struggles. (15)

12. Verbalize positive self-talk regarding educational opportunities. (16)

13. Identify strengths the patient brings to the learning process. (7, 17)

14. Agree to pursue educational assistance to attain reading skills. (7, 11, 18, 19)

15. Follow through on attendance at adult education classes in reading. (19)

16. Make the necessary contacts to investigate enrollment in high school or GED classes. (12, 20)

17. Make contact with agencies that offer vocational assessment and training. (12, 20, 21)

18. State commitment to obtain further academic or vocational training. (11, 22)

7. Administer testing or refer patient to an educational specialist to be tested for learning style, cognitive strengths, and to establish or rule out a learning disability.

8. Refer for or perform psychological assessment for Attention Deficit Disorder. (See ADD—Adult chapter in this *Planner.*)

9. Refer for medication evaluation to treat ADD.

10. Monitor medication effects as to compliance, effectiveness, and side effects.

11. Encourage patient to implement the recommendations of the educational, psychological, and medical evaluations.

12. Give encouragement and verbal affirmation when appropriate to patient as he/she works to increase his/her educational level.

13. Assist patient in the development of strategies for handling his/her fears and anxieties in learning situations (e.g., deep breathing, muscle relaxation, positive self-talk, etc.).

14. Ask patient to list the negative messages he/she has had in learning situations from teachers, parents, and peers, and to process list with therapist.

19. Attend classes consistently to obtain further academic or vocational training. (12, 23)

__. _____

_____

__. _____

_____

__. _____

_____

15. Facilitate patient's openness regarding shame or embarrassment surrounding lack of reading ability, educational achievement, or vocational skill.

16. Reframe negative self-talk in light of testing results or overlooked accomplishments.

17. Assist patient in identifying his/her realistic academic strengths.

18. Assess the patient's reading deficits.

19. Refer patient to resources for learning to read.

20. Provide patient with information regarding community resources available for adult education for GED, high school completion, and vocational skill training.

21. Assign patient to make preliminary contact with vocational and/or educational training agencies and report back regarding the experience.

22. Elicit a commitment to pursue further academic or vocational training.

23. Monitor and support attendance at educational or vocational classes.

—. _____
   _____

—. _____
   _____

—. _____
   _____

DIAGNOSTIC SUGGESTIONS

Axis I: V62.3   Academic Problem
             V62.2   Occupational Problem
             315.2   Disorder of Written Expression
             315.00   Reading Disorder

             _____   _____

Axis II: V.62.89 Borderline Intellectual Functioning
             317   Mild Mental Retardation

             _____   _____
             _____   _____

FAMILY CONFLICT

BEHAVIORAL DEFINITIONS

1. Constant or frequent conflict with parents and/or siblings.
2. A family that is not a stable source of positive influence or support since family members have little or no contact with each other.
3. Ongoing conflict with parents, which is characterized by parents fostering dependence and patient feeling that parents are overly involved in patient's life.
4. Residence with parents and inability to live independently for more than a brief period.
5. Long periods of noncommunication with parents, and description of self as the "black sheep."
6. Remarriage of two parties, both of whom bring children into the marriage from previous relationships.

—. _____
   _____

—. _____
   _____

—. _____
   _____

LONG-TERM GOALS

1. Resolve fear of rejection, low self-esteem, and/or oppositional defiance by resolving conflicts developed in the family of origin and understanding their connection to current life.
2. Begin the process of emancipating from parents in a healthy way by making arrangements for independent living.

3. Decrease the level of present conflict with parents while beginning to let go of or resolving past conflicts with them.
4. Achieve a reasonable level of family connectedness and harmony where members support, help, and are concerned for each other.
5. Become a reconstituted/blended family unit that is functional and bonded to each other.

—. _____
_____
_____
—. _____
_____
—. _____
_____

SHORT-TERM OBJECTIVES

1. Describe the conflicts and the causes of conflicts between self and parents. (1, 2)

2. Attend and participate in family therapy sessions where the focus is on controlled, reciprocal, respectful communication of thoughts and feelings. (3, 8)

3. Demonstrate an increased openness in the family unit between all members by each sharing his/her thoughts and feelings. (4, 5)

4. Identify own role in the family conflicts. (2, 6, 7)

5. Verbalize an increased awareness of the family dynamics and how the family system reinforces the status quo. (4, 5, 7, 8)

THERAPEUTIC INTERVENTIONS

1. Give verbal permission for patient to have and express own feelings, thoughts, and perspectives in order to foster a sense of autonomy from family.

2. Explore the nature of the conflicts and their perceived causes.

3. Conduct family therapy sessions with patient and parents to facilitate healthy communication, conflict resolution, and emancipation process.

4. Conduct a family session in which a process genogram is formed that is complete with members, patterns of interaction, rules, and secrets.

5. Facilitate each family member in expressing their concerns, fears, and expec-

6. Identify factors that reinforce dependence on the family and discover how to overcome them. (9, 10)

7. Increase the number of positive family interactions by planning activities such as bowling, fishing, playing table games, or doing work projects. (11, 12, 13)

8. Verbally describe his/her understanding of the role played by family relationship stress in triggering substance abuse or relapse. (14, 15)

9. Identify the role that chemical dependence behavior plays in triggering family conflict. (16)

10. Identify ways in which the parental team can be strengthened. (17, 18, 19)

11. Parents report how both are involved in the home and parenting process. (17, 19, 20)

12. Decrease the number and frequency of conflictual interactions between parent(s) and child by using "time out" to deescalate the conflict. (21, 22)

13. Report an increase in resolving conflicts with parent by talking calmly and assertively rather than aggressively and defensively. (23, 24)

14. Increase structure within the family. (17, 25, 26)

tations regarding becoming a more functional family unit.

6. Confront patient when he/she is not taking responsibility for self in family conflict and reinforce patient for owning responsibility for his/her role in the conflict.

7. Ask patient to read the book *Making Peace With Your Parents* (Bloomfield and Felder) and select concepts from it to begin using in conflict resolution.

8. Teach all family members that resistance to change in styles of relating to one another is usually high and that change takes concerted effort by all members.

9. Ask patient to make a list of ways he/she is dependent on parents.

10. For each factor that promotes patient's dependence on parents, develop a constructive plan to reduce that dependence.

11. Refer family for an experiential weekend at a center for family education to build skills and confidence in working together. (Consider a physical confidence class with low or high ropes courses, etc.)

12. Ask parents to read *Raising Self Reliant Children* (Glenn and Nelsen), *Between Parent and Child*

15. Each family member repre-
    sents pictorially and then
    describes his/her role in the
    family. (27, 28)
16. Family members negotiate
    with each other to plan and
    implement a family activity.
    (29)
17. Family members report a
    desire for and vision of a
    new sense of connectedness.
    (30, 31)
18. Increase level of indepen-
    dent functioning—that is,
    finding and keeping a job,
    saving money, socializing
    with friends, finding own
    housing, and so on. (23, 32)
19. State goal and plan for
    emancipation. (33)

___. _____
    _____
___. _____
    _____
___. _____
    _____

(Ginott), *Between Parent
and Teenager* (Ginott), or
similar work, and process
key concepts gathered from
their reading with thera-
pist.
13. Assist patient in developing
    a list of positive family ac-
    tivities that promote har-
    mony. Schedule such
    activities into the family
    calendar.
14. Help patient see the trig-
    gers for chemical depen-
    dence relapse in the family
    conflicts.
15. Ask patient to read *It Will
    Never Happen To Me*
    (Black) or *On The Family*
    (Bradshaw) and process key
    family issues from the read-
    ing that are triggers for
    him/her and process each
    with therapist.
16. Confront patient with the
    need for chemical depen-
    dence treatment and ar-
    range for such a focus. (See
    Chemical Dependence and
    Chemical Dependence—
    Relapse chapters in this
    Planner.)
17. Refer parents to a parent-
    ing group to help expand
    their understanding of chil-
    dren and to build skills in
    handling behavior and
    discipline.
18. Direct parents to attend a
    Toughlove group for support
    and feedback on their
    situation.

19. Train parents in the Barkley Method (see *Defiant Children* by Barkley) of understanding and managing defiant and oppositional behavior.

20. Read and process in family therapy session the fable "Raising Cain" or "Cinderella" (see *Friedman's Fables* by Friedman).

21. Assign parents to read *Siblings Without Rivalry* (Faber and Mazlish) and process key concepts with therapist. Then choose and implement a way to start intervening with their children.

22. Train parents in *1-2-3 Magic* (Phelan) or *Parenting with Love and Logic* (Cline and Fay) approach to discipline for young children, then monitor and readjust their implementation as necessary.

23. Confront emotional dependence and avoidance of economic responsibility that promotes continuing pattern of living with parents.

24. Use role-playing, role reversal, modeling, and behavioral rehearsal to help patient develop specific constructive ways to resolve conflict with parents.

25. Assist parents in developing rituals such as dinner times, bedtime readings, weekly family activity

times, and so on that will
provide structure and promote bonding.

26. Assist parents in increasing
structure within the family
by setting times for eating
meals together, limiting
number of visitors, setting a
lights-out time, establishing
a phone call cutoff time,
curfew time, "family meeting" time, and so on.

27. Conduct a family session in
which all members bring
self-produced drawings of
themselves in relationship
to the family. Each will talk
about what they've brought
and then have the picture
placed in an album.

28. Ask the family to make a
collage of cut-out pictures
from magazines depicting
"family" through their eyes
and design a coat of arms
that will signify the blended
unit.

29. In a family therapy session
assign the family the task
of planning and going on an
outing or activity. Then in
the following session process the experience with the
family, giving positives
where appropriate.

30. Conduct a session with all
new family members in
which a genogram is con-
structed gathering the history of both families and
that visually shows how the
new family connection
will be.

31. Assign parents to read the book *Changing Families* (Fassler, Lash, and Ives) at home with family and report their impressions in family therapy session.

32. Probe patient's fears surrounding emancipation.

33. Assist patient in developing a plan for a healthy and responsible emancipation from parents that is, if possible, complete with their blessing.

__. _____
   _____

__. _____
   _____

__. _____
   _____

DIAGNOSTIC SUGGESTIONS

Axis I:	300.4	Dysthymic Disorder
	300.00	Anxiety Disorder NOS
	312.34	Intermittent Explosive Disorder
	303.90	Alcohol Dependence
	304.20	Cocaine Dependence
	304.80	Polysubstance Dependence
	_____	_____
	_____	_____
Axis II:	301.7	Antisocial Personality Disorder
	301.6	Dependent Personality Disorder
	301.83	Borderline Personality Disorder
	301.9	Personality Disorder NOS
	_____	_____
	_____	_____

FEMALE SEXUAL DYSFUNCTION

BEHAVIORAL DEFINITIONS

1. Consistently very low desire for or no pleasurable anticipation of sexual activity.
2. Strong avoidance of and/or repulsion to any and all sexual contact in spite of a relationship of mutual caring and respect.
3. Recurrent lack of usual physiological response of sexual excitement and arousal (genital lubrication and swelling).
4. Consistent lack of subjective sense of enjoyment and pleasure during sexual activity.
5. Persistent delay in or absence of reaching orgasm after achieving arousal and in spite of sensitive sexual pleasuring by a caring partner.
6. Genital pain before, during, or after sexual intercourse.
7. Consistent or recurring involuntary spasm of the vagina that prohibits penetration for sexual intercourse.

—. _____
_____

—. _____
_____

—. _____
_____

LONG-TERM GOALS

1. Increase desire for and enjoyment of sexual activity.
2. Attain and maintain physiological excitement response during sexual intercourse.

3. Reach orgasm with a reasonable amount of time, intensity, and focus given to sexual stimulation.
4. Eliminate pain and promote subjective pleasure before, during, and after sexual intercourse.
5. Eliminate vaginal spasms that prohibit penile penetration during sexual intercourse and achieve a sense of relaxed enjoyment of coital pleasure.

—. _____
   _____

—. _____
   _____

—. _____
   _____

SHORT-TERM OBJECTIVES

1. Share thoughts and feelings regarding relationship with sexual partner. (1, 2)

2. Openly discuss with partner conflicts and unfulfilled needs in the relationship that lead to anger and emotional distance. (1, 2)

3. Discuss sexual attitudes learned in family of origin experiences. (3, 4, 5)

4. Provide a detailed sexual history that explores all experiences that influence sexual attitudes, feelings, and behavior. (3, 4, 5, 6)

5. State an understanding of how religious training negatively influenced sexual thoughts, feelings, and behavior. (4, 5, 6)

THERAPEUTIC INTERVENTIONS

1. Assess the relationship with sexual partner as to level of harmony and fulfillment.

2. Direct conjoint sessions that focus on conflict resolution, expression of feelings, and sex education.

3. Probe family of origin history for causes of inhibition, guilt, fear, or repulsion.

4. Obtain a detailed sexual history that examines current adult sexual functioning as well as childhood and adolescent experiences, level and sources of sexual knowledge, typical sexual practices and frequency of them, medical history, and use of mood-altering substances.

6. Describe negative feelings regarding sexual experiences of childhood or adolescence. (3, 4, 5, 7)

7. Verbalize a resolution of feelings regarding sexual trauma or abuse experiences. (7, 8)

8. Verbalize an understanding of the role of family of origin experiences in the development of negative sexual attitudes and responses. (3, 4, 5, 6, 9)

9. Verbalize an understanding of the connection between lack of positive sex role model in childhood and current adult sexual dysfunction. (3, 4, 5, 10)

10. Verbalize negative cognitive messages that trigger fears, shame, anger, or grief during sex activity. (11)

11. Verbalize the development of positive and healthy automatic thoughts that mediate relaxed pleasure. (12, 15, 26)

12. Verbalize positive and healthy sexual attitudes. (13, 14, 15)

13. Read and discuss books assigned on human sexuality. (13, 14)

14. State acceptance of sexual feelings and behavior as normal and healthy. (13, 14, 15, 26)

15. Demonstrate healthy and accurate knowledge of sexuality by freely verbalizing

5. Explore role of family of origin in teaching negative attitudes regarding sexuality.

6. Explore role of religious training in reinforcing feelings of guilt and shame surrounding sexual behavior and thoughts.

7. Probe client's history for experience of sexual trauma or abuse.

8. Process emotions surrounding an emotional trauma in the sexual arena. (See chapter on Sexual Abuse in this *Planner*.)

9. Assist patient in developing insight into the role of unhealthy sexual attitudes and experiences of childhood in the development of current adult dysfunction. Press for a commitment to put negative attitudes and experiences in the past while making a behavioral effort to become free from those influences.

10. Explore sex role models patient has experienced in childhood or adolescence.

11. Probe automatic thoughts that trigger negative emotions before, during, and after sexual activity.

12. Train patient in healthy alternative thoughts that will mediate pleasure, relaxation, and disinhibition.

13. Disinhibit and educate the patient by talking freely and respectfully regarding

adequate information of sexual functioning using appropriate terms for sexually related body parts. (13, 14, 15)

16. Abstain from substance abuse patterns that interfere with sexual response. (4, 16)

17. Verbalize an understanding of the role physical disease or medication has on sexual dysfunction. (16, 17, 18)

18. Cooperate with a physician's complete examination and report results. (16, 18)

19. Take medication for sexual arousal disorder as prescribed and report as to its effectiveness and side effects. (19)

20. Discuss feelings of and causes for depression. (1, 7, 20, 21)

21. Verbalize connection between previously failed intimate relationships as to behaviors and emotions that caused failure. (4, 22)

22. Discuss feelings surrounding secret affair and make termination decision on one of the relationships. (1, 23)

23. Openly acknowledge and discuss, if present, lesbian attraction. (4, 11, 23, 24)

24. Practice sensate focus exercises alone and with partner and share feelings associated with activity. (25, 26, 27)

sexual body parts, sexual feelings, and sexual behavior.

14. Assign books (e.g., *Sexual Awareness* by McCarthy and McCarthy, *The Gift of Sex* by Penner and Penner, or *The New Male Sexuality* by Zilbergeld) that provide accurate sexual information and/or outline sexual exercises that disinhibit and reinforce sexual sensate focus.

15. Reinforce patient talking freely, knowledgeably, and positively regarding sexual thoughts, feelings, and behavior.

16. Assess the possible role that substance abuse, diabetes, hypertension, or thyroid disease may have on sexual functioning.

17. Review medications taken by patient with regard to their possible negative side effects on sexual functioning.

18. Refer to a physician for a complete physical to rule out any organic basis for dysfunction.

19. Physician to prescribe medication to overcome sexual arousal disorder (e.g., Viagra or hormone replacement).

20. Assess role of depression in suppressing sexual desire or performance.

21. Refer for antidepressant medication prescription to alleviate depression.

25. Write about sexual feelings and thoughts in a daily journal. (13, 28, 29)

26. Write a journal of sexual fantasies that stimulate sexual arousal. (28, 29)

27. Implement new coital positions and settings for sexual activity that enhance pleasure and satisfaction. (14, 30, 31)

28. Engage in more assertive behaviors that allow for sharing sexual needs, feelings, and desires, behaving more sensuously, and expressing pleasure. (27, 29, 30, 31)

29. Resolve conflicts or develop coping strategies that reduce stress interfering with sexual interest or performance. (1, 20, 32)

30. Discuss low self-esteem issues that impede sexual functioning and verbalize positive self-image. (5, 7, 9, 20, 33)

31. Communicate feelings of threat to partner that are based on perception of partner being too sexually aggressive or too critical. (2, 33, 34)

32. Verbalize a positive body image. (11, 12, 13, 35, 36)

33. Verbalize increasing desire for and pleasure with sexual activity. (19, 20, 30, 31, 37)

22. Explore patient's fears surrounding intimate relationships and whether there is evidence of repeated failure in this area.

23. Discuss any secret sexual affairs that may account for sexual dysfunction with partner.

24. Explore lesbian interest that accounts for heterosexual disinterest.

25. Assign body exploration and awareness exercises that reduce inhibition and desensitize patient to sexual aversion.

26. Assign graduated steps of sexual pleasuring exercises with partner that reduce performance anxiety and focus on experiencing bodily arousal sensations.

27. Give permission for less inhibited, less constricted sexual behavior by assigning body-pleasuring exercises with partner.

28. Assign patient to keep a journal of sexual thoughts and feelings to increase awareness and acceptance of them as normal.

29. Encourage development of an indulgence in sexual fantasies that mediate enhanced sexual desire.

30. Suggest experimentation with coital positions and settings for sexual play that may increase security, arousal, and satisfaction.

34. Report to therapist regarding progress on use of masturbation and vaginal dilator to achieve relaxed comfort with penetration. (25, 29, 38)

35. Practice gradual client-controlled vaginal penetration with partner. (25, 38, 39)

__. _____

_____

__. _____

_____

__. _____

_____

31. Encourage patient to gradually explore role of being more sexually assertive, sensuously provocative, and freely uninhibited in sexual play with partner.

32. Probe stress in areas such as work, extended family, and social relationships that distract patient from sexual desire or performance.

33. Explore fears of inadequacy as a sexual partner that led to sexual avoidance.

34. Explore feelings of threat brought on by perception of partner as sexually aggressive.

35. Assign patient to list assets of her body.

36. Discuss feelings regarding body image, focusing on causes for negativism.

37. Reinforce expressions of desire for and pleasure with sexual activity.

38. Direct the use of masturbation and/or vaginal dilator devices to reinforce relaxation and success surrounding vaginal penetration.

39. Direct patient's sexual partner in sexual exercises that allow for patient-controlled level of genital stimulation and gradually increased vaginal penetration.

___. _____
_____
___. _____
_____
___.)_____
_____

DIAGNOSTIC SUGGESTIONS

Axis I: 302.71   Hypoactive Sexual Desire Disorder
302.79   Sexual Aversion Disorder
302.72   Female Sexual Arousal Disorder
302.73   Female Orgasmic Disorder
302.76   Dyspareunia
306.51   Vaginismus
V61.21   Sexual Abuse of Child (995.5, Victim)
625.8   Female Hypoactive Sexual Desire Disorder
          Due to (Axis III Disorder)
625.0   Female Dyspareunia Due to (Axis III Disorder)
302.70   Sexual Dysfunction NOS

____   _____
____   _____

FINANCIAL STRESS

BEHAVIORAL DEFINITIONS

1. Indebtedness and overdue bills that exceed the ability to meet monthly payments.
2. Loss of income due to unemployment.
3. Reduction in income due to change in employment status.
4. Conflict with spouse over management of money and the definition of necessary expenditures and savings goals.
5. A feeling of low self-esteem and hopelessness that is associated with the lack of sufficient income to cover cost of living.
6. A long-term lack of discipline in money management has led to excessive indebtedness.
7. An uncontrollable crisis (e.g., medical bills, job layoff, etc.) has caused past-due bill balances to exceed ability to make payments.
8. Fear of losing housing because of an inability to meet monthly mortgage payment.
9. A pattern of impulsive spending that does not consider the eventual financial consequences.

__. _____

_____

__. _____

_____

__. _____

_____

LONG-TERM GOALS

1. Establish a clear income and expense budget that will meet bill payment demands.

2. Contact creditors to develop a revised repayment plan for outstanding bills.
3. Gain a new sense of self-worth, one in which the substance of one's value is not attached to the capacity to do things or own things that cost money.
4. Understand personal needs, insecurities, and anxieties that make overspending possible.
5. Achieve an inner strength to say no to one's personal impulses, cravings, and desires which directly or indirectly increase debt irresponsibly.

__. _____
    _____

__. _____
    _____

__. _____
    _____

SHORT-TERM OBJECTIVES

1. Describe the details of the current financial situation. (1, 2, 3)

2. Reconstruct the history of the problem in an attempt to isolate the sources and causes of the excessive indebtedness. (3, 4)

3. Verbalize feelings of depression, hopelessness, and/or shame that are related to financial status. (5, 6)

4. Describe any suicidal impulses that may accompany financial stress. (6, 7)

5. Identify priorities that should control how money is spent. (8)

THERAPEUTIC INTERVENTIONS

1. Provide a supportive, comforting environment by being empathetic, warm, and sensitive to the fact that the topic may elicit guilt, shame, and embarrassment.

2. Explore the patient's current financial situation.

3. Assist patient in compiling a complete list of financial obligations.

4. Assist in identifying, without projection of blame or holding to excuses, the causes for the financial crisis.

6. Describe the family of origin pattern of money management and how that pattern may be impacting own credit crisis. (9)

7. Identify steps to take immediately to deal with expenses exceeding income. (10)

8. Meet with community agency personnel to apply for welfare assistance. (10, 11)

9. Contact church or community agencies that can provide temporary financial assistance. (11)

10. Write a budget that balances income with expenses. (12, 13)

11. Attend a meeting with a credit counselor to gain assistance in budgeting and contacting creditors for establishment of a reasonable repayment plan. (12, 14, 15)

12. Meet with an attorney to help reach a decision regarding filing for bankruptcy. (10, 16)

13. Identify personal traits that make undisciplined spending possible. (17)

14. Acknowledge impulsive spending as part of a general pattern of impulsivity that is based on mood swings. (18)

15. Describe honestly any of own or family member's substance abuse problems

5. Probe feelings of hopelessness or helplessness that may be associated with the financial crisis.

6. Assess the depth or seriousness of the patient's despondency over the financial crisis.

7. Assess the potential risk for suicidal behavior. If necessary, take steps to ensure patient's safety. (See chapter on Suicidal Ideation in this *Planner.*)

8. Ask patient to list priorities that he/she believes should give direction to how money is spent. Process those priorities.

9. Explore family of origin patterns of earning, saving, and spending money, focusing on how those patterns are influencing patient's current financial decisions.

10. Review the need for filing for bankruptcy, applying for welfare, and/or obtaining credit counseling.

11. Direct patient to the proper church or community resources to provide welfare assistance and support him/her in beginning the humbling application process.

12. If financial planning is needed, refer to a professional planner or ask partners to write a current budget and long-range savings and investment plan.

that contribute to financial irresponsibility. (19, 20)

16. Verbalize a plan for seeking employment to raise level of income. (21)

17. Agree to set financial goals and make budgetary decisions with partner, allowing for equal input and balanced control over financial matters. (22, 23)

18. Implement a change in how decisions are made regarding allocation of money that reflects mutual agreement between partners. (23)

19. Keep weekly and monthly records of financial income and expenses. (24)

20. Report each instance of debt resolution as it occurs. (25)

21. Use cognitive and behavioral strategies to control the impulse to make unnecessary and unaffordable purchases. (26, 27, 28, 29, 30)

22. Report instances of control over impulse to spend for unnecessary expenses. (28, 29, 30)

___. _____

_____

___. _____

_____

___. _____

_____

13. Review budget as to reasonableness and completeness.

14. Refer to a nonprofit, no-cost credit counseling service for the development of a budgetary plan of debt repayment.

15. Encourage attendance at all credit counseling sessions and discipline of self to control spending within budgetary guidelines.

16. Refer to an attorney to discuss the feasibility and implications of filing for bankruptcy.

17. Probe for evidence of low self-esteem, need to impress others, loneliness, or depression that may accelerate unnecessary, unwarranted spending.

18. Assess for mood swings that are characteristic of bipolar disorder and could be responsible for careless spending due to impaired judgment of manic phase.

19. Probe for excessive alcohol or other drug use by asking questions from the CAGE or Michigan Alcohol Screening Test (MAST) screening instruments for substance abuse.

20. Explore the possibility of alcohol or drug use by family member or significant other.

21. Assist patient in formulating a plan for a job search.

22. Encourage financial planning that is done as a partnership.

23. Reinforce changes in managing money that reflect compromise, responsible planning, and respectful cooperation with partner.

24. Encourage patient to keep weekly and monthly record of income and outflow. Review records weekly and reinforce responsible financial decision making.

25. Offer praise and ongoing encouragement of debt resolution.

26. Role-play some situations in which the patient must resist the inner temptation to spend beyond reasonable limits, emphasizing positive self-talk that complements self for being disciplined.

27. Role-play some situations in which the patient must resist external pressure to spend beyond what he/she can afford (e.g., friend's invitation to golf or go shopping; child's request for a toy), emphasizing being graciously assertive in refusing the request.

28. Reinforce with praise and encouragement all reports of resisting the urge to overspend.

29. Teach the patient the cognitive strategy of asking self before each purchase: Is this purchase absolutely

necessary? Can we afford
this? Do we have the cash
to pay for this without in-
curring any further debt?

30. Urge patient to avoid all
impulse buying by delaying
every purchase until after
24 hours of thought and by
buying only from a prewritten list of items to buy.

__. _____
_____

__. _____
_____

__. _____
_____

DIAGNOSTIC SUGGESTIONS

Axis I: 296.4x   Bipolar I Disorder, Manic
296.89   Bipolar II Disorder
296.xx   Major Depressive Disorder

_____   _____

Axis II: 301.83   Borderline Personality Disorder
301.7   Antisocial Personality Disorder

_____   _____
_____   _____

GRIEF/LOSS UNRESOLVED

BEHAVIORAL DEFINITIONS

1. Thoughts dominated by loss coupled with poor concentration, tearful spells, and confusion about the future.
2. Serial losses in life (i.e., deaths, divorces, jobs) that led to depression and discouragement.
3. Strong emotional response exhibited when losses are discussed.
4. Lack of appetite, weight loss, and/or insomnia as well as other depression signs that occurred since the loss.
5. Feelings of guilt that not enough was done for the lost significant other or an unreasonable belief of having contributed to the death of significant other.
6. Avoidance of talking on anything more than a superficial level about the loss.
7. Loss of a positive support network due to a geographic move.

—. _____
   _____
—. _____
   _____
—. _____
   _____

LONG-TERM GOALS

1. Begin a healthy grieving process around the loss.
2. Develop an awareness of how the avoidance of grieving has affected life and begin the healing process.
3. Complete the process of letting go of the lost significant other.

4. Resolve the loss and begin renewing old relationships and initiating new contacts with others.

—. _____

_____

—. _____

_____

—. _____

_____

SHORT-TERM OBJECTIVES

1. Identify the losses that have been experienced in life. (1, 2, 3)

2. Verbalize an increased understanding of the steps in the grief process. (3, 4, 5, 6)

3. Identify what stages of grief have been experienced in the continuum of the grieving process. (4)

4. Tell the detailed story of the current loss that is triggering symptoms. (2, 3, 10)

5. Read books on the topic of grief to better understand the experience and increase a sense of hope. (5, 6)

6. Begin verbalizing feelings associated with the loss. (7, 8, 9)

7. Watch videos on the theme of grief and loss to compare personal experience with that of characters in the films (10)

8. Attend a grief support group. (11)

THERAPEUTIC INTERVENTIONS

1. Actively build the level of trust with the patient in individual sessions through consistent eye contact, active listening, unconditional positive regard, and warm acceptance to help increase his/her ability to identify and express thoughts and feelings.

2. Ask patient to elaborate in an autobiography on the circumstances, feelings, and effects of the loss or losses in life.

3. Ask patient to talk to several people about losses in their lives as to how they felt and coped. Process findings.

4. Educate the patient on the stages of the grieving process and answer any questions.

5. Ask patient to read the books *Getting to the Other Side of Grief: Overcoming*

9. Identify how avoiding dealing with the loss has negatively impacted life. (5, 10, 12)

10. Identify how the use of substances has aided the avoidance of feelings associated with the loss. (12, 13)

11. Agree to treatment that focuses on substance abuse that has been used to escape from the pain of grief. (14)

12. Verbalize and resolve feelings of anger or guilt focused on self or deceased loved one that blocks the grieving process. (9, 15, 16, 17, 19)

13. Write letters to lost loved one to express memories and feelings associated with the loss. (17, 18, 19)

14. Acknowledge dependency on lost loved one and begin to refocus life on independent actions to meet emotional needs. (5, 15, 17, 20)

15. Identify causes for feelings of regret associated with actions toward or relationship with the deceased. (21)

16. Express thoughts and feelings about deceased that went unexpressed while deceased was alive. (17, 18, 22, 23)

17. Identify the positive characteristics of the deceased loved one, the positive aspects of the relationship with the deceased loved

the Loss of a Spouse (Zonnebelt-Smeenge and DeVries), *Good Grief* (Westberg), *How Can It Be All Right When Everything Is All Wrong* (Smedes), *How to Survive the Loss of a Love* (Colgrove, Bloomfield, and McWilliams), *When Bad Things Happen to Good People* (Kushner), or another book on grief and loss.

6. Ask parents to read *The Bereaved Parent* (Schiff) and to process with therapist the key themes gleaned from the reading that are significant to parent's loss of a child.

7. Assign patient to keep a daily grief journal to be shared in therapy sessions.

8. Ask patient to bring pictures or mementos connected with the loss to a session and talk about them with therapist.

9. Assist patient in identifying and expressing feelings connected with the loss.

10. Ask patient to watch the films *Terms of Endearment, Dad, Ordinary People,* or similar film that focuses on loss and grieving and then discuss how characters cope with loss and express their grief.

11. Ask patient to attend a grief/loss support group and report to therapist how he/she felt about attending.

one, and how these things may be remembered. (24, 25)

18. Decrease statements and feelings of being responsible for the loss. (15, 16, 26)

19. Decrease time spent daily focused on the loss. (27, 28)

20. Develop and enact act(s) of penitence. (15, 21, 26, 29)

21. Attend and participate in a family therapy session focused on each member sharing his/her experience with grief. (30)

22. Implement acts of spiritual faith as a source of comfort and hope. (31)

—. _____
_____

—. _____
_____

—. _____
_____

12. Ask patient to list ways avoidance of grieving has negatively impacted his/her life.

13. Assess the role of substance abuse as an escape from the pain of grief.

14. Arrange for chemical dependence treatment so grief issues can be faced while patient is clean and sober. (See Chemical Dependence chapter in this *Planner.*)

15. Explore feelings of anger or guilt that surround the loss, helping patient understand the sources for such feelings.

16. Encourage patient to forgive self and/or deceased to resolve feelings of guilt or anger. Recommend books like *Forgive and Forget* (Smedes).

17. Ask patient to write a letter to lost person describing fond memories, painful and regretful memories, and how he/she currently feels. Read the letter in session.

18. Assign patient to write to the deceased loved one with a special focus on feelings associated with the last meaningful contact with the person.

19. Assist patient in identifying and expressing feelings connected with the loss.

20. Assist patient in identifying how he/she depended upon significant other, expressing

and resolving the accompanying feelings of abandonment and being left alone.

21. Assign patient to make a list of all the regrets he/she has concerning the loss and to process list with therapist.

22. Conduct an empty chair exercise with the patient where he/she focuses on expressing to lost loved one imagined in the empty chair what he/she never said while that loved one was present.

23. Assign patient to visit the grave of loved one to "talk to" deceased and ventilate feelings.

24. Ask patient to list the most positive aspects of and memories about the relationship with the lost loved one.

25. Assist patient in developing rituals (e.g., place memorium in newspaper on anniversary of death or volunteer time to a favorite cause of the deceased loved one) that will celebrate the memorable aspects of the deceased loved one and his/her life.

26. Use a Rational Emotive Therapy approach to confront patient statements of responsibility for the loss and compare them to reality-based facts.

27. Develop a grieving ritual with an identified feeling state (e.g., dress in all dark colors, preferably black, to indicate deep sorrow) on which the patient may focus near the anniversary of the loss. Process what he/she received from the ritual.

28. Suggest that the patient set aside a specific time-limited period each day to focus on mourning the loss. After time period is up the patient will get on with regular daily activities with agreement to put off thoughts until next scheduled time. (Mourning times could include putting on dark clothing and/or sad music, etc. Clothing would be changed when allotted time period is up.)

29. Research with the patient the activities, interests, commitments, loves, and passions of the lost loved one then select an activity (community service connected) to do as a act of penitence for the feelings of failing the departed one in some way. (Period of time should not be less than 1 month with intensity and duration increasing with depth of the perceived offense.)

30. Conduct a family and/or group session with the patient participating where

each member talks about
his/her experience related
to the loss.

31. Encourage the patient to
rely upon his/her spiritual
faith promises, activities
(e.g., prayer, meditation,
worship, music, etc.), and
fellowship as sources of
support.

—. _____

_____

—. _____

_____

—. _____

_____

DIAGNOSTIC SUGGESTIONS

Axis I: 296.2x   Major Depressive Disorder, Single Episode
296.3x   Major Depressive Disorder, Recurrent
V62.82   Bereavement
309.0   Adjustment Disorder with Depressed Mood
309.3   Adjustment Disorder with Disturbance of
         Conduct
300.4   Dysthymic Disorder

_____   _____

_____   _____

IMPULSE CONTROL DISORDER

BEHAVIORAL DEFINITIONS

1. Several episodes of loss of control of aggressive impulses out of proportion to the situation and resulting in assaultive acts or destruction of property.
2. A consistent pattern of acting before thinking that has resulted in numerous negative impacts on his/her life.
3. Overreactivity to mildly aversive or pleasure-oriented stimulation.
4. Excessive shifting from one activity to another and rarely, if ever, completing anything that is started.
5. Difficulty organizing things or self without supervision.
6. Difficulty waiting for things—that is, restless standing in line, talking out over others in a group, and the like.
7. Failure to resist an impulse, desire, or temptation to perform some act that is harmful to self or others.

—. _____
_____

—. _____
_____

—. _____
_____

LONG-TERM GOALS

1. Decrease the frequency of impulsive acts.
2. Reduce the frequency of impulsive behavior and increase the frequency of behavior that is carefully thought out.
3. Reduce thoughts that trigger impulsive behavior and increase self-talk that controls behavior.

4. Learn to stop, think, listen, and plan before acting.

___. _____

_____

___. _____

_____

___. _____

_____

SHORT-TERM OBJECTIVES

1. Identify the impulsive behaviors that have been engaged in over the last six months. (1, 2)

2. List the reasons or rewards that lead to continuation of an impulsive pattern. (3)

3. List the negative consequences that accrue to self and others as a result of impulsive behavior. (4, 5, 6)

4. Keep a log of impulsive behavior and its antecedents, mediators, and consequences. (7)

5. Verbalize a clear connection between impulsive behavior and negative consequences to self and others. (4, 5, 6, 7, 8)

6. Before acting on behavioral decisions, frequently review them with a trusted friend or family member for feedback regarding possible consequences. (9)

THERAPEUTIC INTERVENTIONS

1. Explore and document instances of impulsive behavior.

2. Assist patient in increasing ability to observe self.

3. Ask patient to make a list of positive things he/she gets from impulsive actions and process it with therapist.

4. Assign the patient to list the negative consequences that occurred because of impulsivity.

5. Help patient make connections between his/her impulsivity and negative consequences experienced.

6. Confront denial of responsibility for the impulsive behavior or the negative consequences.

7. Ask patient to keep a log of impulsive acts (time, place, thoughts, what was going on prior to act) and process log with therapist.

7. Identify the thoughts that trigger impulsive behavior. (7, 10)

8. Utilize cognitive methods to control trigger thoughts and reduce impulsive reactions to those trigger thoughts. (11)

9. Describe the role that tension or anxiety plays in triggering impulsive behavior. (3, 7, 12)

10. Use relaxation exercises to control anxiety and reduce consequent impulsive behavior. (13)

11. Utilize behavioral strategies to manage anxiety. (13, 14)

12. Practice the assertive formula, "I feel . . . When you . . . I would prefer it if. . . ." (15)

13. Identify situations where assertiveness has been implemented and describe the consequences. (16)

14. Practice stopping, thinking, listening, and planning before acting. (17)

15. List instances where "stop, think, listen, and plan" has been implemented, citing the positive consequences. (18)

16. Comply with a physician evaluation regarding the necessity for psychopharmacological intervention. (19, 20)

8. Reinforce the verbalized acceptance of responsibility for and connection between impulsive behavior and negative consequences.

9. Conduct a session with spouse/significant other and patient to develop a contract for receiving feedback prior to impulsive acts.

10. Explore past experiences to uncover triggers to impulsive episodes.

11. Teach patient cognitive methods (thought stoppage, thought substitution, reframing, etc.,) for gaining and improving control over impulsive actions.

12. Explore whether impulsive behavior is triggered by anxiety and maintained by anxiety relief rewards.

13. Using relaxation techniques such as progressive relaxation, self-hypnosis, or biofeedback, teach the patient how to relax completely, then have the patient relax whenever he/she feels uncomfortable.

14. Teach the use of positive behavioral alternatives to cope with anxiety (e.g., talking to someone about the stress, taking a time-out to delay any reaction, calling a friend or family member, engaging in physical exercise).

17. Comply with taking all medications as ordered and report as to effectiveness and side effects. (19, 20)

18. Identify rewards that can be enjoyed contingent on suppression of impulsive behavior. (21)

19. Implement a reward system for replacing impulsive actions with reflection or consequences and choosing patient alternatives. (22)

—. _____
   _____

—. _____
   _____

—. _____
   _____

15. Using modeling, role-playing, and behavior rehearsal, show the patient how to use the assertive formula "I feel . . . When you . . . I would prefer it if . . ." in difficult situations.

16. Review implementation of assertiveness and feelings about it as well as the consequences of it.

17. Using modeling, role-playing, and behavior rehearsal, teach the patient how to use "stop, think, listen, and plan" before acting in several current situations.

18. Review the use of "stop, think, listen, and plan" in day-to-day living and identify the positive consequences.

19. Refer and arrange for patient to have a physician evaluation for medication.

20. Monitor patient for compliance, side effects, and overall effectiveness of the medication. Redirect patient when necessary and consult with prescribing physician at regular intervals.

21. Assist patient in identifying rewards that would be effective in reinforcing suppressing impulsive behavior.

22. Assist patient and significant others in developing and putting into effect a reward system for deterring impulsive actions.

—. _____
    _____
—. _____
    _____
—. _____
    _____

DIAGNOSTIC SUGGESTIONS

Axis I: 312.34   Intermittent Explosive Disorder
              312.32   Kleptomania
              312.31   Pathological Gambling
              312.39   Trichotillomania
              312.30   Impulse Control Disorder NOS
              312.33   Pyromania
              310.1   Personality Change Due to (Axis III Disorder)

              _____   _____

Axis II: 301.7   Antisocial Personality Disorder
              301.83   Borderline Personality Disorder

              _____   _____
              _____   _____

INTIMATE RELATIONSHIP CONFLICTS

BEHAVIORAL DEFINITIONS

1. Frequent or continual arguing with spouse or significant other.
2. Lack of communication with spouse or significant other.
3. A pattern of angry projection of responsibility for the conflicts onto the other party.
4. Marital separation.
5. Pending divorce.
6. Involvement in multiple intimate relationships at the same time.
7. Physical and/or verbal abuse in a relationship.
8. A pattern of superficial or no communication, infrequent or no sexual contact, excessive involvement in activities (work or recreation) that allows for avoidance of closeness to spouse.
9. A pattern of repeated broken, conflictual relationships due to personal deficiencies in problem solving, maintaining a trust relationship, or choosing abusive or dysfunctional partners.

—. _____
   _____
—. _____
   _____
—. _____
   _____

LONG-TERM GOALS

1. Accept the termination of the relationship.
2. Develop the necessary skills for effective, open communication, mutually satisfying sexual intimacy, and enjoyable time for companionship within the relationship.

3. Increase awareness of own role in the relationship conflicts.
4. Develop respect for significant other in the relationship.
5. Learn to identify escalating behaviors that lead to abuse.
6. Make a commitment to one intimate relationship at a time.
7. Rebuild positive self-image after acceptance of the rejection associated with the broken relationship.

—. _____
_____

—. _____
_____

—. _____
_____

SHORT-TERM OBJECTIVES

1. Arrange, attend, and actively participate in conjoint sessions with spouse or significant other. (1)

2. Identify the positive aspects of patient's present relationship. (2, 3, 4)

3. Identify the causes for past and present conflicts within the relationship. (5, 6)

4. Each partner identifies his/her own role in the conflicts and changes he/she must make to improve the relationship. (5, 7, 8)

5. Each partner lists the changes he/she would like from the other to improve the relationship. (9)

6. Each partner makes a commitment to attempt to change specific behaviors that have been identified by self or other. (10, 11)

THERAPEUTIC INTERVENTIONS

1. Facilitate conjoint sessions with significant other with focus on increasing communication and learning problem-solving skills.

2. Assist patient in identifying behaviors that focus on relationship building.

3. Assign a list of positive things about the relationship and positive things about the significant other.

4. Assign the couple to spend the time between sessions noticing and recording in journals the positive things that are present in the relationship. Patients are not to show their journal material to the other until the next session with the therapist.

5. Explore current, ongoing conflicts regarding the relationship.

7. Increase the frequency and quality of the communication with spouse/significant other. (12, 13, 14, 15)

8. Reduce critical complaining by reframing each complaint into a polite request. (16)

9. Express thoughts and feelings regarding the relationship in a direct, nonaggressive manner. (16, 17)

10. Identify and verbalize expectations both partners have for the relationship. (18)

11. Verbally recognize own responsibility to meet some needs of significant other in the relationship. (8, 10, 19)

12. Utilize new conflict resolution techniques to resolve issues reasonably. (20)

13. Identify a pattern in repeatedly forming destructive intimate relationships. (21, 22)

14. Each partner lists escalating behaviors that often lead to verbal or physical abuse. (23)

15. Both partners agree to a "time-out" signal that either partner may give to stop interaction that may become abusive. (24, 25)

16. Verbalize an agreement to the connection between substance abuse and the conflicts present within the relationship. (26, 27)

6. Assign patient to read the book *The Intimate Enemy* (Bach and Wyden) and process key ideas with therapist.

7. Confront each partner for projection of and avoidance of responsibility for conflicts within the relationship.

8. Ask each partner to make list of changes needed for self to improve relationship.

9. Assign each partner a list of changes the other needs to make to improve the relationship.

10. Seek a commitment from each partner to begin to work on changing specific behaviors on his/her own list and on the list of the partner for him/her.

11. In conjoint sessions, process changes each partner believes are necessary to improve the relationship.

12. Make an assignment to the couple to set aside 10 minutes that are distraction free 2 to 3 times each week during which they can communicate about conflict issues. The couple will practice with therapist during session then do at home. As assignment is completed, explore thoughts, feelings with each partner in following session.

13. Encourage patients to attend a skills-based marital/ relationship seminar such

17. Chemically dependent partner agrees to pursue treatment and seek clean and sober living. (27)

18. Identify the message behind a partner's infidelity. (28, 29)

19. Identify the causes for and consequences of one partner's infidelity. (30, 31)

20. Discuss the level of closeness/distance desired in a relationship and how this may relate to fears of intimacy. (32, 33, 34)

21. Share family and childhood experiences with each other to increase understanding and empathy. (35, 36)

22. Increase time spent in enjoyable contact with spouse. (37)

23. Initiate verbal and physical affection behaviors toward spouse. (38, 39)

24. Identify or rule out sexual dysfunction. (40, 41, 42)

25. Identify patterns of sexual behavior, beliefs, and attitudes that exist in each partner's family of origin. (43)

26. Commit to the establishment of healthy, mutually satisfying sexual attitudes and behavior that is not a reflection of destructive earlier experiences. (44)

27. Verbalize the various feelings associated with grieving the loss of the relationship (e.g., denial, guilt,

as PREP and then continue to practice the skills obtained there at home and in conjoint sessions.

14. Assist each partner in clarifying communication and expression of feelings within sessions.

15. Assign patient to talk daily with spouse about prechosen, nonemotional, nonconflictual topics.

16. Ask the couple to reframe a complaint into a request and to seek agreement from the partner to meet this request.

17. Train in assertiveness or refer patient to a group that will educate and facilitate assertiveness skills via lectures and assignments.

18. Confront irrational beliefs and unrealistic expectations regarding relationships and then assist couple in adopting more realistic beliefs and expectations of each other and of the relationship.

19. Teach both partners the key concept that mutually satisfying relationships necessitate each partner being willing at some times to sacrifice his/her own needs and desires to chose to meet the needs and desires of the other.

20. Teach the couple conflict resolution techniques like "Do's & Don'ts List" and

anger, embarrassment, fear, and loneliness). (33, 45, 46)

28. Express plans as to how to cope with loneliness. (47, 48, 49)

__. _____
_____

__. _____
_____

__. _____
_____

"Fair Fighting Steps" (Bach and Wyden) and have them practice these techniques in session and at home.

21. Probe family of origin history of each partner to see patterns of destructive intimate relationship interaction repeating themselves in the present relationship.

22. Gather personal history of each partner as to previous dysfunctional intimate relationships.

23. Ask each partner to make a list of escalating behaviors that occur prior to abusive behavior.

24. Assist partners in identifying a clear verbal or behavioral signal to be used by either partner to terminate interaction immediately if either fears impending abuse.

25. Solicit a firm agreement from both partners that the "time-out" signal will be responded to favorably without debate.

26. Explore the role of substance abuse in precipitating conflict and/or abuse in the relationship.

27. Solicit agreement for substance abuse treatment for the chemically dependent partner. (See the Chemical Dependence chapter in this *Planner.*)

28. Using Emily Brown's "Five Degrees For Affairs" in her book *Patterns of Infidelity and Their Treatment,* assist the couple in identifying the message behind the infidelity.

29. Assign patients to read *After the Affair* (Abrahms-Spring) and then process key concepts gathered from the reading in conjoint sessions with therapist.

30. Explore needs that motivate maintaining multiple intimate relationships.

31. Discuss the consequences to self and others that result from multiple intimate relationships.

32. Direct patients to read *Getting the Love You Want* (Hendrix) and/or attend an Imago workshop to create relationship skills.

33. Explore and clarify feelings associated with loss of the relationship.

34. Explore each partner's fears regarding getting too close and feeling vulnerable to hurt, rejection, or abandonment.

35. Assist couple in doing an Imago exercise where each shares with the other childhood wounds they experienced to expand understanding and sharing. (Format: Recall the incident; tell what you enjoyed about being with parents;

next, tell how you were hurt by parents; and last, tell what you wanted from them but never got. Repeat for each incident.)

36. Assign each client to complete a genogram and then share in conjoint session his/her genogram with the other to promote greater empathy and awareness concerning each other.

37. Assist in identifying and planning rewarding, shared social/recreational activities with partner.

38. Encourage patients to read *Passionate Marriage* (Schnarch) and/or attend a couples enrichment or retreat weekend led by Schnarch and begin implementing and practicing key concepts gathered from the reading or the experience.

39. Diffuse resistance surrounding initiating affectionate or sexual interactions with spouse.

40. Explore with couple the nature of their sexual relationship to determine or rule out any sexual issues. (See chapters on Female Sexual Dysfunction and Male Sexual Dysfunction in this *Planner.*)

41. Make referral to a physician who specializes in treating sexual dysfunction for an evaluation.

42. Gather from each partner in the relationship a thorough sexual history to determine areas of strength and to identify areas of dysfunction.

43. Create with the couple in a conjoint session a sexual genogram which identifies sex patterns of behavior, activities, and beliefs for the couple and their extended family.

44. Assist each partner to commit to attempting to develop healthy, mutually satisfying sexual beliefs, attitudes, and behavior that is independent of previous childhood, personal, or family training or experience.

45. Refer patient to a support group or divorce seminar to assist in resolving the loss and in adjusting to new life.

46. Assign patient to read *How to Survive the Loss of a Love* (Colgrove, Bloomfield, and McWilliams) and to process key concepts with therapist.

47. Help, support, and encourage patient in his/her adjustment to living alone and being single.

48. Make patient aware of the community resources and social opportunities that are available to him/her.

49. Assist patient in developing a specific plan regarding building new social relationships to overcome withdrawal and fear of rejection.

—. _____

_____

—. _____

_____

—. _____

_____

DIAGNOSTIC SUGGESTIONS

Axis I:	312.34	Intermittent Explosive Disorder
	309.0	Adjustment Disorder with Depressed Mood
	309.24	Adjustment Disorder with Anxiety
	300.4	Dysthymic Disorder
	300.00	Anxiety Disorder NOS
	311	Depressive Disorder NOS
	309.81	Posttraumatic Stress Disorder
	_____	_____
	_____	
Axis II:	301.20	Schizoid Personality Disorder
	301.81	Narcissistic Personality Disorder
	301.9	Personality Disorder NOS
	_____	_____
	_____	_____

LEGAL CONFLICTS

BEHAVIORAL DEFINITIONS

1. Legal charges pending.
2. Parole or probation subsequent to legal charges.
3. Legal pressure that has been central to the decision to enter treatment.
4. A long history of criminal activity leading to numerous incarcerations.
5. Chemical dependence resulting in several arrests and current court involvement.
6. Pending divorce accompanied by emotional turmoil.
7. Fear of loss of freedom due to current legal charges.

__. _____
   _____
__. _____
   _____
__. _____
   _____

LONG-TERM GOALS

1. Accept and responsibly respond to the mandates of court.
2. Understand how chemical dependence has contributed to legal problems and accept the need for recovery.
3. Accept responsibility for decisions and actions that have led to arrests and develop higher moral and ethical standards to govern behavior.
4. Internalize the need for treatment so as to change values, thoughts, feelings and behavior to a more prosocial position.

5. Become a responsible citizen in good standing within the community.
6. Accept and adapt to the uncontrollable actions of the court.

—. _____
   _____
   _____

—. _____
   _____
   _____

—. _____
   _____
   _____

SHORT-TERM OBJECTIVES

1. Describe the behavior that led to current involvement with the court system. (1)
2. Obtain counsel and meet to make plans for resolving legal conflicts. (2)
3. Make regular contact with court officers to fulfill sentencing requirements. (3)
4. Verbalize the role drug and/or alcohol abuse has played in legal problems. (4, 5)
5. State a desire to remain abstinent. (6)
6. Maintain sobriety in accordance with rules of probation/parole. (6, 7)
7. Verbalize and accept responsibility for the series of decisions and actions that eventually led to illegal activity. (8, 9)
8. State values that affirm behavior within the boundaries of the law. (8, 9, 10)

THERAPEUTIC INTERVENTIONS

1. Explore the patient's behavior that led to legal conflicts and assess whether it fits a pattern of antisocial behavior. (See Antisocial Behavior chapter in this *Planner*.)
2. Encourage and facilitate the patient in meeting with an attorney to discuss plans for resolving legal issues.
3. Monitor and encourage patient to keep appointments with court officers.
4. Explore issue of chemical dependence and how it may have contributed to legal conflicts.
5. Confront denial of chemical dependence by reviewing various negative consequences of addiction.
6. Reinforce need for a plan for recovery and sobriety as means of improving judgement and control over behavior. (See Chemical

9. Verbalize how the emotional state of anger, frustration, helplessness, or depression has contributed to illegal behavior. (11, 13)

10. Identify the causes for negative emotional state that was associated with illegal actions. (12, 13, 14)

11. Identify cognitive distortions that foster antisocial behavior. (15)

12. Implement positive self-talk that fosters positive behavior. (16)

13. Attend an anger control group. (17)

14. Identify ways to meet life needs (i.e., social and financial) without resorting to illegal activities. (18, 19)

15. Attend class to learn how to successfully seek employment. (20)

16. Verbalize an understanding of the importance of honesty in building trust in others and esteem for self. (21)

17. Develop and implement a plan for restitution for illegal activity. (21, 22)

__. _____
    _____
__. _____
    _____
__. _____
    _____

Dependence chapter in this *Planner*.)

7. Monitor and reinforce sobriety, using physiological measures to confirm, if advisable.

8. Assist patient in clarification of values that allow illegal actions.

9. Confront denial and projection of responsibility onto others for own illegal actions.

10. Discuss values associated with respecting legal boundaries and the rights of others as well as the consequences of crossing these boundaries.

11. Probe negative emotional states that could contribute to illegal behavior.

12. Explore causes for underlying negative emotions that consciously or unconsciously foster criminal behavior.

13. Refer patient for ongoing counseling to deal with emotional conflicts and antisocial impulses. (See Antisocial Behavior, Anger Management, or Depression chapters in this *Planner*.)

14. Interpret antisocial behavior that is linked to current or past emotional conflicts to foster insights and resolution.

15. Assess and clarify cognitive belief structures that foster illegal behavior.

16. Restructure cognitions to those that foster keeping of legal boundaries and respecting the rights of others.

17. Refer patient to an impulse or anger management group.

18. Explore with patient ways he/she can meet social and financial needs without involvement with illegal activity (e.g., employment, further education or skill training, spiritual enrichment group, etc.).

19. Educate patient on the difference between antisocial and prosocial behaviors. Then help make concrete plans on how to show respect for the law, help others, and work regularly.

20. Refer patient to an ex-offender center for assistance in obtaining employment.

21. Help the patient understand the importance of honesty in building trust and self-respect.

22. Assist patient in seeing the importance of restitution to self-worth and then help in developing a plan to provide restitution for the results of his/her behavior.

—. _____
_____
—. _____
_____
—. _____
_____

DIAGNOSTIC SUGGESTIONS

Axis I: 304.20   Cocaine Dependence
303.90   Alcohol Dependence
312.32   Kleptomania
V71.01   Adult Antisocial Behavior
309.3   Adjustment Disorder with Disturbance of
Conduct

_____   _____
_____   _____

Axis II: 301.7   Antisocial Personality Disorder

_____   _____
_____   _____

LOW SELF-ESTEEM

BEHAVIORAL DEFINITIONS

1. Inability to accept compliments.
2. Self-disparaging remarks; sees self as unattractive, worthless, a loser, a burden, unimportant; takes blame easily.
3. Lack of pride in grooming.
4. Difficulty in saying no to others; assumes not being liked by others.
5. Fear of rejection of others, especially peer group.
6. Lack of any goals for life and setting of inappropriately low goals for self.
7. Inability to identify positive things about self.
8. Uncomfortable in social situations, especially in larger groups.

—. _____
_____
—. _____
_____
—. _____
_____

LONG-TERM GOALS

1. Elevate self-esteem.
2. Develop a consistent, positive self-image.
3. Demonstrate improved self-esteem through more pride in appearance, more assertiveness, greater eye contact, and identification of positive traits in self-talk messages.

—. _____
   _____
—. _____
   _____
—. _____
   _____

SHORT-TERM OBJECTIVES

1. Acknowledge feeling less competent than most others. (1, 2)

2. Increase awareness of self-disparaging statements. (3, 4)

3. Increase insight into the historical and current sources of low self-esteem. (5, 6)

4. Identify accomplishments that would improve self-image and verbalize a plan to achieve those goals. (7, 8, 9)

5. List own unmet needs for self-fulfillment. (10)

6. Articulate a plan to be proactive in trying to get identified needs met. (11, 12)

7. Decrease the verbalized fear of rejection while increasing statements of self-acceptance. (5, 13, 14, 15)

8. Decrease the frequency of negative self-descriptive statements and increase frequency of positive self-

THERAPEUTIC INTERVENTIONS

1. Actively build the level of trust with the patient in individual sessions through consistent eye contact, active listening, unconditional positive regard, and warm acceptance to help increase his/her ability to identify and express feelings.

2. Explore patient's assessment of self.

3. Confront and reframe patient's self-disparaging comments.

4. Assist the patient in becoming aware of how he/she expresses or acts out negative feelings about himself/herself.

5. Help patient become aware of the fear of rejection and its connection with past rejection or abandonment experiences.

6. Discuss, emphasize, and interpret incidents of abuse (emotional, physical, and sexual) and how they have impacted feelings about self.

descriptive statements.
(4, 13, 15)

9. Identify positive traits
and talents about self.
(13, 14, 16, 17)

10. Increase eye contact with
others. (16, 18, 19)

11. Demonstrate an increased
ability to identify and
express personal feelings.
(20, 21)

12. Identify any secondary gain
that is received by speaking
negatively about self and
refusing to take any risks.
(22, 23)

13. Take responsibility for daily
grooming and personal
hygiene. (24)

14. Positively acknowledge
verbal compliments from
others. (16, 19, 25)

15. Increase frequency of
assertive behaviors.
(11, 12, 26)

16. Form realistic, appropriate,
and attainable goals for self
in all areas of life. (7, 27)

17. Take verbal responsibility
for accomplishments with-
out discounting. (14, 25, 28)

18. Identify negative self-talk
messages used to reinforce
low self-esteem. (3, 9, 29)

19. Use positive self-talk messages to build self-esteem.
(14, 30, 31)

20. Increase the frequency of
speaking up with confidence
in social situations.
(18, 19, 32, 33)

7. Help patient analyze goals
to make sure they are realistic and attainable.

8. Assign self-esteem-building
exercises from a workbook
such as *The Building Blocks
of Self-Esteem* (Shapiro)
or a selected individual
exercise.

9. Ask patient to complete and
process an exercise in the
book *Ten Days to Self-
Esteem!* (Burns).

10. Assist the patient in becoming capable of identifying
and verbalizing needs.

11. Conduct a conjoint or family
therapy session in which
patient is supported in expression of unmet needs.

12. Assist patient in developing
a specific action plan to get
needs met.

13. Ask the patient to make one
positive statement about
self daily and record it on a
chart or in a journal.

14. Verbally reinforce the use of
positive statements of confidence and accomplish-
ments.

15. Assist the patient in developing self-talk as a way of
boosting his/her confidence
and positive self-image.

16. Assign mirror exercises of
patient talking positively
about self.

17. Reinforce patient's positive
self-descriptive statements.

—. _____
_____

—. _____
_____

—. _____
_____

18. Confront patient when he/she is observed avoiding eye contact with others.

19. Assign patient to make eye contact with whomever he/she is speaking to.

20. Assign patient to keep a journal of feelings on a daily basis.

21. Assist patient in identifying and labeling emotions.

22. Teach patient the meaning and power of secondary gain in maintaining negative behavior patterns.

23. Assist patient in identifying how self-disparagement and avoidance of risk taking could bring secondary gain (e.g., praise from others, others taking over responsibilities, etc.)

24. Monitor and when necessary give feedback to patient on his/her grooming and hygiene.

25. Assign patient to be aware and acknowledge graciously (without discounting) praise and compliments from others.

26. Train in assertiveness or refer patient to a group that will educate and facilitate assertiveness skills via lectures and assignments.

27. Assign patient to make a list of goals for various areas of life and a plan for steps toward goal attainment.

28. Ask patient to list accomplishments. Process the integration of these into self-image.

29. Help patient identify distorted, negative beliefs about self and the world.

30. Assign patient to read *What to Say When You Talk to Yourself* (Helmstetter) and process key ideas with therapist.

31. Reinforce use of more realistic, positive messages to self in interpreting life events.

32. Use role-playing and behavioral rehearsal to improve patient's social skills in greeting people and carrying conversation.

33. Recommend that patient read *Shyness* (Zimbardo).

___. _____
    _____

___. _____
    _____

___. _____
    _____

DIAGNOSTIC SUGGESTIONS

Axis I:	300.23	Social Phobia
	300.4	Dysthymic Disorder
	296.xx	Major Depressive Disorder
	296.xx	Bipolar I Disorder
	296.89	Bipolar II Disorder
	_____	_____
	_____	_____

MALE SEXUAL DYSFUNCTION

BEHAVIORAL DEFINITIONS

1. Consistently very low or no pleasurable anticipation of or desire for sexual activity.
2. Strong avoidance of and/or repulsion to any and all sexual contact in spite of a relationship of mutual caring and respect.
3. Recurrent lack of usual physiological response of sexual excitement and arousal (attaining and/or maintaining an erection).
4. Consistent lack of subjective sense of enjoyment and pleasure during sexual activity.
5. Persistent delay in or absence of reaching ejaculation after achieving arousal and in spite of sensitive sexual pleasuring by a caring partner.
6. Genital pain before, during, or after sexual intercourse.

__. _____
   _____

__. _____
   _____

__. _____
   _____

LONG-TERM GOALS

1. Increase desire for and enjoyment of sexual activity.
2. Attain and maintain physiological excitement response during sexual intercourse.
3. Reach ejaculation with a reasonable amount of time, intensity, and focus to sexual stimulation.

4. Eliminate pain and achieve a presence of subjective pleasure before, during, and after sexual intercourse.

—. _____

_____

—. _____

_____

—. _____

_____

SHORT-TERM OBJECTIVES

1. Share thoughts and feelings regarding relationship with sexual partner. (1, 2)

2. Openly discuss with partner conflicts and unfulfilled needs in the relationship that lead to anger and emotional distance. (1, 2)

3. Discuss sexual attitudes learned in family of origin experiences. (3, 4, 5)

4. Provide a detailed sexual history that explores all experiences that influence sexual attitudes, feelings, and behavior. (3, 4, 5, 6)

5. State an understanding of how religious training negatively influenced sexual thoughts, feelings, and behavior. (4, 5, 6)

6. Describe negative feelings regarding sexual experiences of childhood or adolescence. (3, 4, 5, 7)

THERAPEUTIC INTERVENTIONS

1. Assess the relationship with sexual partner as to level of harmony and fulfillment.

2. Direct conjoint sessions that focus on conflict resolution, expression of feelings, and sex education.

3. Probe family of origin history for causes of inhibition, guilt, fear, or repulsion.

4. Obtain a detailed sexual history that examines current adult sexual functioning as well as childhood and adolescent experiences, level and sources of sexual knowledge, typical sexual practices and frequency of them, medical history, and use of mood-altering substances.

5. Explore role of family of origin in teaching negative attitudes regarding sexuality.

6. Explore role of religious training in reinforcing feelings of guilt and shame sur-

7. Verbalize a resolution of feelings regarding sexual trauma or abuse experiences. (7, 8)

8. Verbalize an understanding of the role of family of origin experiences in the development of negative sexual attitudes and responses. (3, 4, 5, 6, 9)

9. Verbalize an understanding of the connection between lack of positive sex role model in childhood and current adult sexual dysfunction. (3, 4, 5, 10)

10. Verbalize negative cognitive messages that trigger fears, shame, anger, or grief during sexual activity. (11)

11. Verbalize the development of positive and healthy automatic thoughts that mediate relaxed pleasure. (12, 15, 26)

12. Verbalize positive and healthy sexual attitudes. (13, 14, 15)

13. Read and discuss books assigned on human sexuality. (13, 14)

14. State acceptance of sexual feelings and behavior as normal and healthy. (13, 14, 15, 26)

15. Demonstrate healthy and accurate knowledge of sexuality by freely verbalizing accurate information regarding sexual functioning using appropriate terms for

rounding sexual behavior and thoughts.

7. Probe patient's history for experience of sexual trauma or abuse.

8. Process emotions surrounding an emotional trauma in the sexual arena. (See chapter on Sex Abuse in this *Planner*.)

9. Assist patient in developing insight into the role of unhealthy sexual attitudes and experiences of childhood in the development of current adult dysfunction. Press for a commitment to put negative attitudes and experiences in the past while making a behavioral effort to become free from those influences.

10. Explore sex role models patient has experienced in childhood or adolescence.

11. Probe automatic thoughts that trigger negative emotions before, during, and after sexual activity.

12. Train patient in healthy alternative thoughts that will mediate pleasure, relaxation, and disinhibition.

13. Disinhibit and educate the patient by talking freely and respectfully regarding sexual body parts, sexual feelings, and sexual behavior.

14. Assign books (e.g., *Sexual Awareness* by McCarthy and McCarthy, *The Gift of*

sexually related body parts. (13, 14, 15)

16. Abstain from substance abuse patterns that interfere with sexual response. (4, 16)

17. Verbalize an understanding of the role physical disease or medication has on sexual dysfunction. (16, 17, 18)

18. Cooperate with a physician's complete examination and report results. (16, 18)

19. Take medication for impotence as ordered and report as to effectiveness and side effects. (19)

20. Discuss feelings of and causes for depression. (1, 7, 20, 21)

21. Verbalize connection between previously failed intimate relationships as to behaviors and emotions that caused failure. (4, 22)

22. Discuss feelings surrounding secret affair and make termination decision on one of the relationships. (1, 23)

23. Openly acknowledge and discuss, if present, homosexual attraction. (4, 11, 23, 24)

24. Practice sensate focus exercises alone and with partner and share feelings associated with activity. (25, 26, 27)

25. Write about sexual feelings and thoughts in a daily journal. (13, 28, 29)

Sex by Penner and Penner, or *The New Male Sexuality* by Zilbergeld) that provide accurate sexual information and/or outline sexual exercises that disinhibit and reinforce sexual sensate focus.

15. Reinforce patient talking freely, knowledgeably, and positively regarding sexual thoughts, feelings, and behavior.

16. Assess the possible role that substance abuse, diabetes, hypertension, or thyroid disease may have on sexual functioning.

17. Review medications taken by patient with regard to their possible negative side effects on sexual functioning.

18. Refer to a physician for a complete physical to rule out any organic basis for dysfunction.

19. Refer to a physician for evaluation regarding a prescription of medication to overcome impotence (e.g., Viagra).

20. Assess role of depression in suppressing sexual desire or performance.

21. Refer for antidepressant medication prescription to alleviate depression.

22. Explore patient's fears surrounding intimate relationships and whether there is evidence of repeated failure in this area.

26. Write a journal of sexual fantasies that stimulate sexual arousal. (28, 29)

27. Implement new coital positions and settings for sexual activity that enhance pleasure and satisfaction. (14, 30, 31)

28. Engage in more assertive behaviors that allow for sharing sexual needs, feelings, and desires, behaving more sensuously and expressing pleasure. (27, 29, 30, 31)

29. Resolve conflicts or develop coping strategies that reduce stress interfering with sexual interest or performance. (1, 20, 32)

30. Discuss low self-esteem issues that impede sexual functioning and verbalize positive self-image. (5, 7, 9, 20, 33)

31. Communicate feelings of threat to partner that are based on perception of partner being too sexually aggressive or too critical. (2, 33, 34)

32. Implement the squeeze technique during sexual intercourse and report on success in slowing premature ejaculation and feelings about self and the procedure. (33, 35)

33. Verbalize increasing desire for and pleasure with sexual activity. (19, 20, 30, 31, 36)

23. Discuss any secret sexual affairs that may account for sexual dysfunction with partner.

24. Explore homosexual interest that accounts for heterosexual disinterest.

25. Assign body exploration and awareness exercises that reduce inhibition and desensitize patient to sexual aversion.

26. Assign graduated steps of sexual pleasuring exercises with partner that reduce performance anxiety and focus on experiencing bodily arousal sensations.

27. Give permission for less inhibited, less constricted sexual behavior by assigning body-pleasuring exercises with partner.

28. Assign patient to keep a journal of sexual thoughts and feelings to increase awareness and acceptance of them as normal.

29. Encourage development of an indulgence in sexual fantasies that mediate enhanced sexual desire.

30. Suggest experimentation with coital positions and settings for sexual play that may increase security, arousal, and satisfaction.

31. Encourage patient to gradually explore role of being more sexually assertive, sensuously provocative, and

___. _____
_____

___. _____
_____

___. _____
_____

freely uninhibited in sexual play with partner.

32. Probe stress in areas such as work, extended family, and social relationships that distract patient from sexual desire or performance.

33. Explore fears of inadequacy as a sexual partner that led to sexual avoidance.

34. Explore feelings of threat brought on by perception of partner as sexually aggressive.

35. Instruct patient and partner in use of squeeze technique to retard premature ejaculation. Process the procedure and feelings about it.

36. Reinforce expressions of desire for and pleasure with sexual activity.

___. _____
_____

___. _____
_____

___. _____
_____

DIAGNOSTIC SUGGESTIONS

Axis I:

302.71	Hypoactive Sexual Desire Disorder
302.79	Sexual Aversion Disorder
302.72	Male Erectile Disorder
302.74	Male Orgasmic Disorder
302.76	Dyspareunia
302.75	Premature Ejaculation
608.89	Male Hypoactive Sexual Disorder Due to (Axis III Disorder)
607.84	Male Erectile Disorder Due to (Axis III Disorder)
608.89	Male Dyspareunia Due to (Axis III Disorder)
302.70	Sexual Dysfunction NOS
V61.21	Sexual Abuse of Child (995.5, Victim)
_____	_____
_____	_____

MANIA OR HYPOMANIA

BEHAVIORAL DEFINITIONS

1. Loquaciousness or pressured speech.
2. Flight of ideas or reports of thoughts racing.
3. Grandiosity and/or persecutory beliefs.
4. Decreased need for sleep often with little or no appetite.
5. Increased motor activity or agitation.
6. Poor attention span and easily distracted.
7. Loss of normal inhibition leading to impulsive, pleasure-oriented behavior without regard for painful consequences.
8. Bizarre dress and grooming.
9. Expansive mood that can easily turn to impatience and irritable anger if behavior is blocked or confronted.
10. Lack of follow-through in projects even though energy is very high since behavior lacks discipline and goal-directedness.

__. _____
   _____
   _____
__. _____
   _____
   _____
__. _____
   _____

LONG-TERM GOALS

1. Reduce psychic energy and return to normal activity levels, good judgement, stable mood, and goal-directed behavior.
2. Reduce agitation, impulsivity, and pressured speech while achieving sensitivity to the consequences of behavior and having more realistic expectations.

3. Talk about underlying feelings of low self-esteem or guilt and fears of rejection, dependency, and abandonment.
4. Achieve controlled behavior, moderated mood, and more deliberative speech and thought process through psychotherapy and medication.

—. _____
_____
—. _____
_____
—. _____
_____

SHORT-TERM OBJECTIVES

1. Describe feelings and thoughts about self, own abilities, and future plans. (1, 2, 3)
2. Describe mood state, energy level, amount of control over thoughts, and sleeping pattern. (1, 2, 3)
3. Cooperate with psychiatric evaluation as to need for medication and/or hospitalization to stabilize mood and energy. (2, 3, 4)
4. Take psychotropic medications as directed. (4, 5)
5. Begin to demonstrate trust in the therapy relationship by sharing fears about dependency, loss, and abandonment. (6, 7, 8, 9)
6. Achieve mood stability, becoming slower to react with anger, less expansive, and more socially appropriate and sensitive. (4, 10)

THERAPEUTIC INTERVENTIONS

1. Explore patient for classic signs of mania: pressured speech, impulsive behavior, euphoric mood, flight of ideas, reduced need for sleep, inflated self-esteem, and high energy.
2. Assess stage of elation: hypomanic, manic, or psychotic.
3. Arrange for or continue hospitalization if patient is judged to be potentially harmful to self or others, or unable to care for own basic needs.
4. Arrange for psychiatric evaluation for pharmacotherapy (e.g., lithium carbonate or Depakote).
5. Monitor the patient's reaction to the medication (e.g., side effects and effectiveness).

7. Verbalize grief, fear, and anger regarding real or imagined losses in life. (7, 8, 11, 12)

8. Differentiate between real and imagined losses, rejections, and abandonments. (8, 12)

9. Acknowledge the low self-esteem and fear of rejection that underlie the braggadocio. (9, 10, 13)

10. Identify the causes for the low self-esteem and abandonment fears. (9, 13)

11. Terminate self-destructive behaviors such as promiscuity, substance abuse, and the expression of overt hostility or aggression. (14, 15, 16, 17)

12. Speak more slowly and be more subject focused. (18, 19)

13. Dress and groom in a less attention-seeking manner. (2, 20, 21)

14. Verbalize the acceptance of and peace with dependency needs. (6, 7, 22)

15. Identify positive traits and behaviors that build genuine self-esteem. (23)

16. Decrease grandiose statements and express self more realistically. (10, 19, 22, 24)

17. Be less agitated and distracted—that is, able to sit quietly and calmly for 30 minutes. (4, 25)

6. Pledge to be there consistently to help, listen to, and support the patient.

7. Explore the patient's fears of abandonment by sources of love and nurturance.

8. Probe real or perceived losses in the patient's life.

9. Probe the causes for the patient's low self-esteem and abandonment fears in the family of origin history.

10. Confront the patient's grandiosity and demandingness gradually but firmly.

11. Review ways to replace the losses and put them in perspective.

12. Help the patient differentiate between real and imagined, actual and exaggerated losses.

13. Explore the stressors that precipitate the patient's manic behavior (e.g., school failure, social rejection, or family trauma).

14. Repeatedly focus on the consequences of behavior to reduce thoughtless impulsivity.

15. Facilitate impulse control by using role-playing, behavioral rehearsal, and role reversal to increase sensitivity to consequences of behavior.

16. Calmly listen to expressions of hostility while setting limits on aggressive or impulsive behavior.

18. Sleep about 5 hours or more per night. (2, 4, 5, 18, 26)

19. Report more control over thoughts and a slower thinking process. (2, 4, 5, 18, 27)

20. Report staying focused on a single activity to completion. (2, 4, 5, 18, 28)

21. Verbalize an understanding that behavior and judgment were under poor control during manic phase. (29)

22. Verbalize acceptance of the need for ongoing supportive treatment and medication because without it a destructive, manic swing could redevelop. (30)

23. Family of patient express their feelings regarding patient's behavior and mental illness. (31)

24. Family of patient verbalize an understanding of the serious nature of patient's illness, its behavioral manifestations, and the need for continuing treatment. (32)

—. _____

_____

—. _____

_____

—. _____

_____

17. Set limits on manipulation or acting out by making clear rules and establishing clear consequences for breaking rules.

18. Provide structure and focus for the patient's thoughts and actions by regulating the direction of conversation and establishing plans for behavior.

19. Verbally reinforce slower speech and more deliberate thought process.

20. Encourage and reinforce appropriate dress and grooming.

21. Assist patient in setting reasonable limits on behavior.

22. Interpret the fear and insecurity underlying the patient's braggadocio, hostility, and denial of dependency.

23. Assist the patient in identifying strengths and assets to build self-esteem and confidence.

24. Encourage patient to share feelings at a deeper level to facilitate openness and intimacy in relationships, counteracting denial and superficiality.

25. Reinforce increased control over hyperactivity and help patient set goals and limits on agitation.

26. Monitor patient's sleep pattern and encourage steady return to 5 or more hours sleep per night.

27. Monitor patient's energy level and reinforce increased control over behavior, pressured speech, and expression of ideas.

28. Reinforce reports of behavior that is more focused on goal attainments and less distractable.

29. Explore patient's understanding of his/her illness and reinforce a realistic appraisal of loss of judgement and impulsivity.

30. Teach patient his/her need for ongoing care of a condition that is usually chronic in nature and often misleads a patient into thinking there is no need for medication or therapy.

31. Meet with family to allow ventilation of their feelings of guilt, shame, fear, concern, confusion, or anger regarding patient's behavior.

32. Meet with family to educate them regarding the illness and emphasize the need for ongoing treatment.

__. _____

_____

__. _____

_____

__. _____

_____

DIAGNOSTIC SUGGESTIONS

Axis I:	296.xx	Bipolar I Disorder
	296.89	Bipolar II Disorder
	301.13	Cyclothymic Disorder
	295.70	Schizoaffective Disorder
	296.80	Bipolar Disorder NOS
	310.1	Personality Change Due to (Axis III Disorder)
	_____	_____
	_____	_____

MEDICAL ISSUES

BEHAVIORAL DEFINITIONS

1. A diagnosed serious medical condition that needs attention and has an impact on daily living (e.g., high blood pressure, asthma, seizures, diabetes, heart disease, cancer, or cirrhosis).
2. Constant chronic pain that is debilitating and depressing.
3. A medical condition for which the patient is under a physician's care.
4. A positive test for HIV (human immunodeficiency virus).
5. AIDS (acquired immune deficiency syndrome).
6. Medical complications secondary to chemical dependence.
7. Psychological or behavioral factors that influence the course of the medical condition.
8. History of neglecting his/her physical and medical health.

__. _____

_____

__. _____

_____

__. _____

_____

LONG-TERM GOALS

1. Medically stabilize physical condition.
2. Alleviate acute medical condition.
3. Accept chronic medical condition with proper medical attention given to it.
4. Resolve physical symptoms.

5. Accept the role of psychological or behavioral factors in development of medical condition and focus on resolution of these factors.
6. Take responsibility for maintaining physical health and well-being.
7. Establish chemical dependence recovery that leads to improved physical health.

—. _____
_____
—. _____
_____
—. _____
_____

SHORT-TERM OBJECTIVES

1. Comply totally with doctor's orders for tests, medications, limitations, and/or treatments. (1, 2, 3, 4)

2. Demonstrate responsibility by taking prescribed medication(s) consistently and on time. (4, 5)

3. Report as to treatment effectiveness and side effects. (4, 5)

4. Verbalize an increased understanding of medical condition. (5, 6, 7)

5. Decrease frequency of verbal denial regarding medical condition while increasing frequency of verbal acceptance. (6, 7, 8)

6. Verbalize an increased knowledge of how proper nutrition can have a positive impact on medical condition. (3, 9)

THERAPEUTIC INTERVENTIONS

1. Make any necessary arrangements required for patient to obtain the medical services needed.

2. Refer patient to physician for complete physical.

3. Help the patient understand his/her medical problem and the need to cooperate with doctor's recommendations.

4. Monitor treatment effectiveness and document patient's follow-through on doctor's orders; redirect when patient is failing to comply.

5. Consult with physician and review doctor's orders with patient.

6. Provide to patient any appropriate literature that will increase understanding of his/her medical condition.

7. Identify how chemical dependency has negatively impacted medical condition. (10, 11)

8. Maintain a life of sobriety that supports recovery from medical condition. (11)

9. Acknowledge any high-risk behaviors associated with sexually transmitted disease (STD). (12, 13)

10. Accept the presence of an STD or HIV and follow through with medical treatment. (8, 13, 14, 15)

11. Identify emotional effects of medical condition. (16)

12. Identify how emotions and behavior have negatively impacted health. (17, 18)

13. List changes in nutrition and lifestyle that will be implemented to support medical recovery. (9, 10, 18, 19)

14. Implement an exercise program that is tailored to medical condition. (19)

15. Identify sources of emotional distress that could have a negative impact on physical health. (17, 20, 21)

16. Accept the need for treatment of concomitant emotional problems. (21)

17. Identify fears related to medical treatment and implement steps to overcome such fears. (22, 23)

7. Assign patient to attend a support group related to his/her physical condition and to report the positive aspects of attending to therapist.

8. Confront denial of the seriousness of the medical condition and reinforce acceptance of the condition.

9. Arrange for consultation with dietitian to explain proper nutrition that will enhance medical recovery.

10. Explore and assess the role of chemical abuse on medical condition.

11. Focus treatment on chemical dependence recovery. (See Chemical Dependence chapter in this *Planner*.)

12. Assess patient's behavior for the presence of high risk behaviors (e.g., IV drug use, unprotected sex, gay lifestyle, promiscuity, etc.) related to STD and HIV.

13. Refer patient to public health or physician for STD and/or HIV testing, education, or treatment.

14. Encourage and monitor patient's follow-through on pursuing medical treatment for STD or HIV.

15. Refer to specialized program for patients with HIV.

16. Help patient identify and express his/her feelings connected with medical condition.

—.   _____

        _____

—.   _____

        _____

—.   _____

        _____

17. Teach how lifestyle and emotional distress can have a negative impact on medical condition. Review patient's lifestyle and identify negative factors for physical health.

18. Assign patient to make a list of things he/she could do to help maintain physical health; process list.

19. Refer patient to a physical therapist for assessment and recommendations for an exercise plan that is appropriate for patient's age and medical condition.

20. Explore sources of emotional distress that could make the patient vulnerable to disease and/or reduce the efficacy of treatment.

21. Develop a treatment plan for emotional problems that compromise medical treatment efforts.

22. Help patient identify fears concerning doctors or medical treatment and help him/her work through the blocks, thus allowing him/her to receive necessary care.

23. Process with patient the necessary steps needed in order to ensure that proper medical attention is obtained.

—. _____
   _____
—. _____
   _____
—. _____
   _____

DIAGNOSTIC SUGGESTIONS

Axis I: 304.20   Cocaine Dependence
              303.90   Alcohol Dependence
              307.89   Pain Disorder Associated with Both
                        Psychological Factors and an Axis III Disorder
              307.80   Pain Disorder Associated with Psychological
                        Factors
              300.7   Hypochondriasis
              300.81   Somatization Disorder
              316   Personality Traits Affecting (Axis III Disorder)
              316   Maladaptive Health Behaviors Affecting
                        (Axis III Disorder)
              316   Psychological Symptoms Affecting
                        (Axis III Disorder)

              _____   _____
              _____   _____

OBSESSIVE-COMPULSIVE DISORDER (OCD)

BEHAVIORAL DEFINITIONS

1. Recurrent and persistent ideas, thoughts, or impulses that are viewed as intrusive, senseless, and time-consuming, or that interfere with patient's daily routine, job performance, or social relationships.
2. Failed attempts to ignore or control these thoughts or impulses or neutralize them with other thoughts and actions.
3. Recognition that obsessive thoughts are a product of his/her own mind.
4. Repetitive and intentional behaviors that are done in response to obsessive thoughts or according to eccentric rules.
5. Repetitive and excessive behavior that is done to neutralize or prevent discomfort or some dreaded situation; however, the behavior is not connected in any realistic way with what it is designed to neutralize or prevent.
6. Recognition of repetitive behaviors as excessive and unreasonable.

__. _____

_____

__. _____

_____

__. _____

_____

LONG-TERM GOALS

1. Reduce time involved with or interference from obsessions and compulsions.

2. Function daily at a consistent level with minimal interference from obsessions and compulsions.
3. Resolve key life conflicts and the emotional stress that fuels obsessive-compulsive behavior patterns.
4. Let go of key thoughts, beliefs and past life events in order to maximize time free from obsessions and compulsions.

—. _____

  _____

—. _____

  _____

—. _____

  _____

SHORT-TERM OBJECTIVES

1. Describe nature, history, and severity of obsessive thoughts and/or compulsive behavior. (1)

2. Comply with psychological testing evaluation to assess the nature and severity of the obsessive-compulsive problem. (2)

3. Take medication as prescribed and report any improvement or side effects to therapist. (3, 4)

4. Implement thought-stopping technique to interrupt obsessions. (5)

5. Practice relaxation methods to reduce tension. (6)

6. Utilize biofeedback to improve relaxation ability. (6, 7)

7. Identify key life conflicts that raise anxiety. (8, 9, 10)

THERAPEUTIC INTERVENTIONS

1. Assess the nature, severity, and history of the obsessive-compulsive problems using clinical interview.

2. Arrange for psychological testing to further evaluate the nature and severity of the patient's obsessive-compulsive problem.

3. Arrange for an evaluation for a medication prescription to aid in the control of patient's OCD.

4. Monitor and evaluate patient's medication compliance and the effectiveness or side effects of the medications on level of functioning.

5. Assign thought-stopping technique that cognitively interferes with obsessions by thinking of a stop sign and then a pleasant scene.

8. Verbalize and clarify feelings connected to key life conflicts. (8, 11)

9. Report a decreased level of emotional intensity around conflicts. (6, 7, 10, 11)

10. Verbalize an increased awareness of how he/she believes and thinks. (12)

11. Identify distorted thinking and belief errors and the impact each have on his/her daily functioning. (12, 13, 14)

12. Verbalize positive, reality-based messages that can reduce obsessive and perfectionistic thoughts. (13, 15)

13. Decrease ruminations about death and other perplexing life issues. (12, 13, 16, 17)

14. Implement the Ericksonian task designed to interfere with OCD. (18)

15. Engage in a strategic ordeal to overcome OCD impulses. (19)

16. Develop and implement a daily ritual that interrupts the current pattern of compulsions. (20)

__. _____
_____

__. _____
_____

__. _____
_____

6. Train in relaxation methods (e.g., deep breathing, muscle tension release, positive imagery, etc.) to counteract high anxiety.

7. Administer biofeedback to deepen patient's relaxation skills.

8. Explore patient's life circumstances to help identify key unresolved conflicts.

9. Read with patient the fable "The Friendly Forest" or "Round in Circles" from *Friedman's Fables* (Friedman), and then process using discussion questions.

10. Assign patient to read or read to him/her the story "The Little Clock That Couldn't Tell Time" or "The Little Centipede Who Didn't Know How to Walk" from *Stories for the Third Ear* (Lee Wallas). Process stories with patient.

11. Encourage, support, and assist patient in identifying and expressing feelings related to key unresolved life issues.

12. Ask patient to read "The Perfectionist's Script for Self-Defeat" in *Ten Days to Self-Esteem!* (Burns). Discuss key concepts gathered from the information.

13. Assign patient to complete exercises that focus on cost-benefit analysis (Perfectionist Exercise 1) and distorted thinking (Perfectionist Ex-

ercise 2), from *Ten Days to Self-Esteem!* (Burns). Process exercises.

14. Assist patient in identifying distorted automatic thoughts and beliefs.

15. Assist patient in developing reality-based self-talk as a strategy to help abate his/her obsessive thoughts.

16. Use a Rational Emotive Therapy approach and teach patient to analyze, attack and destroy his/her self-defeating beliefs. Monitor and offer appropriate encouragement.

17. Develop and assign a cognitive/behavioral intervention task that will help disrupt the obsessive-compulsive patterns.

18. Develop and assign an Ericksonian task (e.g., if obsessed with a loss give the patient the task to visit, send a card, or bring flowers to someone who has lost someone) to the patient that is centered around the obsession or compulsion and assess the results with the patient.

19. Create and sell a strategic ordeal that offers a guaranteed cure to the patient for the obsession or compulsion. Note that Haley emphasizes that the "cure" offers an intervention to achieve a goal and is not a promise to cure the patient

at the beginning of therapy. (See *Ordeal Therapy* by Haley.)

20. Help patient create and implement a ritual (e.g., find a job that the patient finds necessary but very unpleasant, and have him/her do this job each time he/she finds thoughts becoming obsessive). Follow up with patient on the outcome of its implementation and make any necessary adjustments.

__. _____
   _____
   _____
__. _____
   _____
   _____
__. _____
   _____

DIAGNOSTIC SUGGESTIONS

Axis I:

300.3	Obsessive-Compulsive Disorder
300.00	Anxiety Disorder NOS
296.xx	Major Depressive Disorder
303.90	Alcohol Dependence
304.10	Sedative, Hypnotic, or Anxiolytic Dependence
_____	_____

Axis II:

301.82	Avoidant Personality Disorder
301.4	Obsessive-Compulsive Personality Disorder
_____	_____
_____	_____

PARANOID IDEATION

BEHAVIORAL DEFINITIONS

1. Extreme or consistent distrust of others generally or someone specifically, without sufficient basis.
2. Expectation of being exploited or harmed by others.
3. Misinterpretation of benign events as having threatening personal significance.
4. Hypersensitivity to hints of personal critical judgement by others.
5. Inclination to keep distance from others out of fear of being hurt or taken advantage of.
6. Tendency to be easily offended and quick to anger; defensive behavior.
7. A pattern of being suspicious of loyalty or fidelity of spouse or significant other without reason.
8. Level of mistrust is obsessional to the point of disrupting patient's daily functioning.

__. _____
_____

__. _____
_____

__. _____
_____

LONG-TERM GOALS

1. Show more trust in others by speaking positively of them and reporting comfort in socializing.
2. Interact with others without defensiveness or anger.

3. Verbalize trust of significant other and eliminate accusations of disloyalty.
4. Report reduced vigilance and suspicion around others as well as more relaxed, trusting, and open interaction.
5. Achieve a level of ability to concentrate on important matters without interference from suspicious obsessions.
6. Appropriate functioning at work, in social activities, and in the community with only minimal interference from distrustful obsessions.

—. _____
   _____
   _____
—. _____
   _____
—. _____
   _____

SHORT-TERM OBJECTIVES

1. Demonstrate a level of trust with therapist by disclosing feelings and beliefs. (1, 2)

2. Identify those people or agencies that are distrusted and why. (3, 8)

3. Agree to collaborate with the therapist in probing feelings of vulnerability. (2, 4, 5)

4. Identify historical sources of feelings of vulnerability. (6)

5. Identify core belief that others are untrustworthy and malicious. (5, 6, 7, 8)

6. Comply with a psychiatric evaluation. (8, 9)

THERAPEUTIC INTERVENTIONS

1. Actively build the level of trust with the patient through consistent eye contact, active listening, unconditional positive regard, and warm acceptance to help increase his/her ability to identify and express feelings.

2. Demonstrate a calm, tolerant demeanor in sessions to decrease patient's fear of others.

3. Explore the nature and extent of paranoia, probing for delusional components.

4. Probe patient's fears of personal inadequacy and vulnerability.

7. Take prescribed medication on a consistent basis as prescribed and report any side effects. (8, 9, 10)

8. Complete a psychological evaluation to assess depth of paranoia. (11)

9. Comply with a neuropsychological evaluation to rule out the possibility of organic etiology. (12)

10. Make verbal connection between fears of others and own feelings of inadequacy. (4, 6, 13)

11. Acknowledge that the belief about others being threatening is based more on subjective interpretation than on objective data. (14, 15, 16)

12. Decrease accusations of others' plans of harm toward self. (9, 14, 17, 19)

13. Verbalize increased trust in others and in the surrounding community. (15, 18, 19)

14. Verbalize trust of significant other and feel relaxed when not in his/her presence. (16, 17, 19, 20)

15. Increase social interaction without fear or suspicion being reported. (18, 19, 20)

—. _____

_____

—. _____

_____

—. _____

_____

5. Interpret patient's fears of own anger as basis for mistrust of others.

6. Explore historical sources of feelings of vulnerability in family of origin experiences.

7. Review social interactions of patient and explore distorted cognitive beliefs operative during interactions.

8. Assess necessity for use of antipsychotic medication to counteract altered thought processes. (See Psychoticism chapter in this *Planner*.)

9. Arrange for an evaluation for psychotropic medications by physician.

10. Monitor patient's medications for compliance, effectiveness, and side effects. Report to prescribing physician on effectiveness and side effects and confront patient when he/she is not taking medication as prescribed.

11. Arrange for a psychological evaluation to assess for possible psychotic process.

12. Refer for or perform neuropsychological evaluation. If organic factors are found refer to a neurologist for consultation.

13. Assist patient in seeing the pattern of distrusting others as related to own fears of inadequacy.

14. Provide alternative explanations for others' behavior that counter patient's pat-

tern of assumption of others' malicious intent.

15. Ask patient to complete a cost-benefit analysis (see *The Feeling Good Handbook* by Burns) around his/her specific fears and process exercise with therapist.

16. Conduct conjoint sessions to assess and reinforce verbalizations of trust toward significant others.

17. Confront irrational distrust of others and provide reality-based data to support trust.

18. Read and process with the patient the story of "Porky the Porcupine" from *Stories for the Third Ear* (Wallas).

19. Encourage the patient to check out his/her beliefs regarding others by assertively verifying conclusions with others.

20. Use role-playing, behavioral rehearsal, and role reversal to increase patient's empathy for others and understanding of the impact of his/her behavior on others.

—. _____
_____

—. _____
_____

—. _____
_____

DIAGNOSTIC SUGGESTIONS

Axis I:	300.23	Social Phobia
	310.1	Personality Change Due to (Axis III Disorder)
	295.30	Schizophrenia, Paranoid Type
	297.1	Delusional Disorder
	_____	_____
	_____	_____
Axis II:	301.0	Paranoid Personality Disorder
	301.22	Schizotypal Personality Disorder
	_____	_____
	_____	_____

PHOBIA-PANIC/AGORAPHOBIA

BEHAVIORAL DEFINITIONS

1. A persistent and unreasonable fear of a specific object or situation that promotes avoidance behaviors because an encounter with the phobic stimulus provokes an immediate anxiety response.
2. Unexpected, sudden, debilitating panic symptoms (shallow breathing, sweating, heart racing or pounding, dizziness, depersonalization or derealization, trembling, chest tightness, fear of dying or losing control, nausea) that have occurred repeatedly resulting in persisting concern about having additional attacks or behavioral changes to avoid attacks.
3. Fear of being in an environment that patient believes may trigger intense anxiety symptoms (panic) and, therefore, patient avoids such situations as leaving home alone, being in a crowd of people, traveling in an enclosed environment.
4. Avoidance or endurance of the phobic stimulus or feared environment with intense anxiety resulting in interference of normal routines or marked distress.
5. Persistence of fear in spite of recognition that the fear is unreasonable.
6. No evidence of agoraphobia.
7. No evidence of panic disorder.

—. _____
_____
—. _____
_____
—. _____
_____

LONG-TERM GOALS

1. Reduce fear so that patient can independently and freely leave home and comfortably be in public environments.
2. Travel away from home in some form of enclosed transportation.
3. Reduce fear of the specific stimulus object or situation that previously provoked immediate anxiety.
4. Eliminate interference in normal routines and remove distress from feared object or situation.
5. Remove panic symptoms and the fear that they will recur without an ability to cope with and control them.

—. _____

_____

—. _____

_____

—. _____

_____

SHORT-TERM OBJECTIVES

1. Verbalize phobic fear and focus on describing the specific stimuli for it. (1, 2, 10)

2. Construct a hierarchy of situations that increasingly evoke anxiety. (3)

3. Become proficient in progressive, deep muscle relaxation and deep breathing. (4, 5)

4. Identify a nonthreatening, pleasant scene that can be utilized to promote relaxation using guided imagery. (6)

5. Cooperate with systematic desensitization to the

THERAPEUTIC INTERVENTIONS

1. Discuss and assess the phobic fear, its depth, and the stimuli for it.

2. Administer a fear survey to further assess the depth and breadth of phobic responses.

3. Direct and assist in construction of a hierarchy of anxiety-producing situations associated with the phobic response.

4. Train in progressive relaxation methods and deep breathing.

5. Utilize biofeedback techniques to facilitate relaxation skills.

anxiety-provoking stimulus object or situation. (3, 4, 5, 6, 7)

6. Undergo in vivo desensitization to the stimulus object or situation. (3, 4, 5, 8)

7. Encounter the phobic stimulus object or situation feeling in control, calm, and comfortable. (8, 9, 22, 23)

8. Identify symbolic significance that the phobic stimulus may have as a basis for fear. (1, 2, 10)

9. Verbalize the separate realities of the irrationally feared object or situation and the emotionally painful experience from the past that has been evoked by the phobic stimulus. (11, 12, 13)

10. Share the feelings associated with past emotionally painful situation that is connected to the phobia. (12, 13)

11. Understand the cognitive beliefs and messages that mediate the anxiety response. (1, 14)

12. Verbalize positive, healthy, and rational self-talk that reduces fear and allows the behavioral encounter with avoided stimuli. (14, 15)

13. Utilize behavioral and cognitive strategies that reduce or eliminate irrational anxiety. (4, 15)

6. Train in guided imagery for anxiety relief.

7. Direct systematic desensitization procedures to reduce phobic response.

8. Assign and/or accompany patient in in vivo desensitization contact with phobic stimulus object or situation.

9. Review and verbally reinforce progress toward overcoming anxiety.

10. Probe, discuss, and interpret possible symbolic meaning of the phobia stimulus object or situation.

11. Clarify and differentiate between the current irrational fear and past emotional pain.

12. Encourage sharing of feelings from past through active listening, positive regard, and questioning.

13. Reinforce insights into past emotional pain and present anxiety.

14. Identify the distorted schemes and related automatic thoughts that mediate anxiety response.

15. Train in revising core schemes using cognitive restructuring techniques.

16. Arrange for the prescription of psychotropic medications to alleviate symptoms.

17. Monitor the patient for compliance, side effects, and overall effectiveness of the

14. Cooperate with an evaluation by a physician for organic causes of symptoms and for psychotropic medication. (16)

15. Responsibly take prescribed psychotropic medication to alleviate phobic anxiety. (16, 17)

16. Describe the history and nature of the panic symptoms. (18, 19)

17. Identify any secondary gain that accrues due to modification of life related to panic. (20)

18. Verbalize an understanding that panic symptoms do not precipitate a serious mental illness, loss of control over self, or heart attack. (21)

19. Practice positive self-talk that reassures self of the ability to endure anxiety symptoms without serious consequences. (22, 25)

20. Utilize deep muscle relaxation and deep breathing skills to terminate panic symptoms and return to a feeling of peace. (4, 5, 23, 24)

21. Commit self to not allowing panic symptoms to take control of life and lead to a consistent avoidance and escape from normal responsibilities and activities. (25, 26)

medication. Consult with the prescribing physician at regular intervals.

18. Explore the symptoms, severity, and history of panic attacks.

19. Explore the nature of any stimulus, thoughts, or situations that precipitate panic.

20. Probe for the presence of secondary gain that reinforces panic symptoms through escape or avoidance mechanisms.

21. Consistently reassure patient of no connection between panic symptoms and heart attack, loss of control over behavior, or serious mental illness ("going crazy").

22. Use modeling and behavioral rehearsal to train patient in positive self-talk that reassures self of ability to work through and endure anxiety symptoms without serious consequences.

23. Train in coping strategies (diversion, deep breathing, positive self-talk, muscle relaxation, etc.) to alleviate symptoms.

24. Encourage the use of deep muscle relaxation and deep breathing skills to manage panic symptoms.

25. Urge patient to keep focus on external stimuli and behavioral responsibilities rather than being preoccu-

—. _____

_____

—. _____

_____

—. _____

_____

pied with internal focus on physiological changes.

26. Support patient in follow-through with work, family, and social activities rather than escaping or avoiding them to focus on panic.

—. _____

_____

—. _____

_____

—. _____

_____

DIAGNOSTIC SUGGESTIONS

Axis I: 300.01   Panic Disorder without Agoraphobia
300.21   Panic Disorder with Agoraphobia
300.22   Agoraphobia without History of Panic Disorder
300.29   Specific Phobia
_____   _____
_____   _____

POSTTRAUMATIC STRESS
DISORDER (PTSD)

BEHAVIORAL DEFINITIONS

1. Exposure to actual or threatened death or serious injury that resulted in an intense emotional response of fear, helplessness, or horror.
2. Intrusive, distressing thoughts or images that recall the traumatic event.
3. Disturbing dreams associated with the traumatic event.
4. A sense that the event is reoccurring, as in illusions or flashbacks.
5. Intense distress when exposed to reminders of the traumatic event.
6. Physiological reactivity when exposed to internal or external cues that symbolize the traumatic event.
7. Avoidance of thoughts, feelings, or conversations about the traumatic event.
8. Avoidance of activity, places, or people associated with the traumatic event.
9. Inability to recall some important aspect of the traumatic event.
10. Lack of interest and participation in significant activities.
11. A sense of detachment from others.
12. Inability to experience the full range of emotions, including love.
13. A pessimistic, fatalistic attitude regarding the future.
14. Sleep disturbance.
15. Irritability.
16. Lack of concentration.
17. Hypervigilance.
18. Exaggerated startle response.
19. Symptoms have been present for more than one month.
20. Sad or guilty affect and other signs of depression.
21. Alcohol and/or drug abuse.
22. Suicidal thoughts.

23. A pattern of interpersonal conflict, especially in intimate relation-
    ships.
24. Verbally and/or physically violent threats or behavior.
25. Inability to maintain employment due to authority/coworker con-
    flict or anxiety symptoms.

__. _____

   _____

__. _____

   _____

__. _____

   _____

LONG-TERM GOALS

1. Reduce the negative impact that the traumatic event has had on
   many aspects of life and return to pretrauma level of functioning.
2. Develop and implement effective coping skills to carry out normal
   responsibilities and participate constructively in relationships.
3. Recall the traumatic event without becoming overwhelmed with
   negative emotions.
4. Terminate the destructive behaviors that serve to maintain escape
   and denial while implementing behaviors that promote healing,
   acceptance of the past events, and responsible living.

__. _____

   _____

__. _____

   _____

__. _____

   _____

SHORT-TERM OBJECTIVES

1. Cooperate with psychological testing to assess for symptoms of PTSD. (1)

2. Identify the symptoms of PTSD that have caused distress and impaired functioning. (2, 3, 4)

\ 3. Describe the traumatic event in as much detail as possible. (5, 6)

\ 4. Describe the feelings that were experienced at the time of the trauma. (6)

5. Identify how PTSD symptoms have affected personal relationships, functioning at work or school, and social/recreational life. (7)

6. Provide honest and complete information for a chemical dependence biopsychosocial history. (8, 9)

7. Verbalize a recognition that mood-altering chemicals were used as the primary coping mechanism to escape from stress or pain, and that their use resulted in negative consequences. (10, 11)

8. Consent to treatment for chemical dependence. (12)

9. Identify instances of the loss of control of anger. (13)

10. Verbalize an awareness of and implement anger control techniques. (14)

THERAPEUTIC INTERVENTIONS

1. Administer or refer for administration of psychological testing to assess for the presence and strength of PTSD symptoms (e.g., MMPI-2, Impact of Events Scale, PTSD Symptom Scale, or Mississippi Scale for Combat Related PTSD).

2. Ask patient to identify how the traumatic event has negatively impacted his/her life.

3. Use the Clinician Administered PTSD Scales (CAPS-1) to assess PTSD status.

4. Ask patient to list and then rank order of the strength of his/her symptoms of PTSD.

ı 5. Gently and sensitively explore the recollection of the facts of the traumatic incident.

6. Explore the patient's emotional reaction at the time of the trauma.

7. Explore the effect that the PTSD symptoms have had on personal relationships, functioning at work or school, and social/recreational life.

8. Assess for the presence of chemical dependence as a means of escape from negative emotions (e.g., fear, guilt, rage, etc.) associated with the trauma.

11. Verbalize an awareness of how PTSD develops and its impact on self and others. (15)

12. Practice and implement relaxation training as a coping mechanism for tension, panic, stress, anger, and anxiety. (16, 17)

13. Implement a regular exercise regimen as a stress release technique. (18, 19)

14. Report increased comfort and ability to talk and/or think about the traumatic incident without emotional turmoil. (20, 21, 22, 23, 26)

15. Identify negative self-talk and catastrophizing that is associated with past trauma and current stimulus triggers for anxiety. (22)

16. Replace negative, self-defeating thinking with positive, accurate, self-enhancing self-talk. (23)

17. Approach actual stimuli (in vivo) that trigger memories and feelings associated with past trauma, staying calm by using relaxation techniques and positive self-talk. (24)

18. Sleep without being disturbed by dreams of the trauma. (16, 17, 18, 19, 25)

19. Cooperate with eye movement desensitization and reprocessing (EMDR) technique to reduce emotional reaction to the traumatic event. (26)

9. Complete a family and personal biopsychosocial history focusing on substance abuse.

10. Probe the sense of shame, guilt, and low self-worth that has resulted from substance abuse and its consequences.

11. Use the biopsychosocial history to help the patient understand the familial, emotional, and social factors that contributed to the development of chemical dependence.

12. Refer or treat for chemical dependence. (See Chemical Dependence chapter in this *Planner*.)

13. Assess for instances of poor anger management that has lead to threats or actual violence causing damage to property and/or injury to people.

14. Teach anger management control techniques. (See Anger Management chapter in this *Planner*.)

15. Refer for didactic sessions or teach the patient the facts about trauma and its impact on survivors and their subsequent adjustment.

16. Teach deep muscle relaxation methods along with deep breathing and positive imagery to induce relaxation.

20. Participate in group therapy session focused on PTSD. (27)

21. Cooperate with an evaluation for medication intervention. (28)

22. Take medication as prescribed and report as to the effectiveness and side effects. (29)

23. Participate in conjoint and/or family therapy sessions. (30)

24. Describe any dissociative symptoms associated with a reaction to the trauma. (31)

25. Verbalize an understanding of the negative impact PTSD has had on vocational functioning and cooperate with treatment for vocational conflicts. (32)

26. Verbalize the symptoms of depression, including any suicidal ideation. (33)

27. Verbalize hopeful and positive statements regarding the future. (34, 35)

__. _____
_____

__. _____
_____

__. _____
_____

17. Utilize EMG biofeedback to increase patient's depth of relaxation.

18. Develop and encourage a routine of physical exercise.

19. Recommend that the patient read and implement programs from *Exercising Your Way to Better Mental Health* (Leith).

20. Utilize gradual exposure to the traumatic event through systematic desensitization and guided imagery to reduce emotional reactivity to the traumatic event.

21. Explore in detail patient's feelings surrounding the traumatic incident, allowing for a gradual reduction in the intensity of the emotional response with repeated retelling.

22. Explore the negative self-talk that is associated with the past trauma and the predictions of unsuccessful coping or catastrophizing.

23. Help patient make a list of his/her negative self-defeating thinking and replace each thought with self-enhancing self-talk.

24. Encourage patient to approach previously avoided stimuli that trigger thoughts and feelings associated with the past trauma. Urge use of relaxation, deep breathing, and positive self-talk during approach to stimulus.

25. Monitor patient's sleep pattern and encourage use of relaxation and positive imagery as aids to sleep. (See Sleep Disturbance chapter in this *Planner.*)

26. Utilize eye movement desensitization and reprocessing (EMDR) technique to reduce emotional reactivity to traumatic event.

27. Refer patient to or conduct group therapy sessions where the focus is on sharing traumatic events and its effects with other PTSD survivors.

28. Assess the need for medication (e.g., selective serotonin reuptake inhibitors) and arrange for prescription, if appropriate.

29. Monitor and evaluate medication compliance and the effectiveness of the medications on patient's level of functioning.

30. Conduct family and conjoint sessions to facilitate healing of hurt caused by symptoms of PTSD.

31. Assess for dissociative symptoms (flashbacks, memory loss, identity disorder, etc.) and treat or refer for treatment. (See Dissociation chapter in this *Planner.*)

32. Explore vocational history and treat vocational issues as appropriate. (See Vocational Stress chapter in this *Planner.*)

33. Assess the depth of depression and suicide potential and treat appropriately, taking the necessary safety precautions as indicated. (See Depression and Suicidal Ideation chapters in this *Planner*.)

34. Assist in developing an awareness of cognitive messages that reinforce hopelessness and helplessness.

35. Reinforce positive, reality-based cognitive messages that enhance self-confidence and increase adaptive action.

__. _____
    _____

__. _____
    _____

__. _____
    _____

DIAGNOSTIC SUGGESTIONS

Axis I:	309.81	Posttraumatic Stress Disorder
	300.14	Dissociative Identity Disorder
	300.6	Depersonalization Disorder
	300.15	Dissociative Disorder NOS
	309.xx	Adjustment Disorder
	V61.21	Physical Abuse of Child (995.5, Victim)
	V61.1	Physical Abuse of Adult (995.5, Victim)
	V61.21	Sexual Abuse of Child (995.5, Victim)
	V61.1	Sexual Abuse of Adult (995.81, Victim)
	308.3	Acute Stress Disorder
	304.80	Polysubstance Dependence
	305.0	Alcohol Abuse
	303.90	Alcohol Dependence

	304.30	Cannabis Dependence
	304.20	Cocaine Dependence
	304.0	Opioid Dependence
	296.xx	Major Depression
	_____	_____
	_____	_____
Axis II:	301.83	Borderline Personality Disorder
	301.9	Personality Disorder NOS
	_____	_____
	_____	_____

PSYCHOTICISM

BEHAVIORAL DEFINITIONS

1. Bizarre content of thought (delusions of grandeur, persecution, reference, influence, control, somatic sensations, or infidelity).
2. Illogical form of thought/speech (loose association of ideas in speech, incoherence; illogical thinking; vague, abstract, or repetitive speech; neologisms, perseverations, clanging).
3. Perception disturbance (hallucinations, primarily auditory but occasionally visual or olfactory).
4. Disturbed affect (blunted, none, flattened, or inappropriate).
5. Lost sense of self (loss of ego boundaries, lack of identity, blatant confusion).
6. Volition diminished (inadequate interest, drive, or ability to follow a course of action to its logical conclusion; pronounced ambivalence or cessation of goal-directed activity).
7. Relationship withdrawal (withdrawal from involvement with external world and preoccupation with egocentric ideas and fantasies, alienation feelings).
8. Psychomotor abnormalities (marked decrease in reactivity to environment; various catatonic patterns such as stupor, rigidity, excitement, posturing, or negativism; unusual mannerisms or grimacing).

—. _____
_____

—. _____
_____

—. _____
_____

LONG-TERM GOALS

1. Control or eliminate active psychotic symptoms such that supervised functioning is positive and medication is taken consistently.
2. Significantly reduce or eliminate hallucinations and/or delusions.
3. Eliminate acute, reactive, psychotic symptoms and return to normal functioning in affect, thinking, and relating.

—. _____

—. _____

—. _____

SHORT-TERM OBJECTIVES

1. Describe the type and history of the psychotic symptoms. (1, 2, 3)
2. Patient or significant other gives family history of serious mental illness. (4)
3. Accept and understand that distressing symptoms are due to mental illness. (5, 6)
4. Understand the necessity for taking antipsychotic medications and agree to cooperate with prescribed care. (7, 8)
5. Take antipsychotic medications consistently with or without supervision. (8)
6. Accept the need for a supervised living environment. (9, 10)
7. Describe history of not providing for own basic needs

THERAPEUTIC INTERVENTIONS

1. Demonstrate acceptance through calm, nurturing manner, good eye contact, and active listening.
2. Assess pervasiveness of thought disorder through clinical interview and/or psychological testing.
3. Determine if psychosis is of a brief reactive nature or long term with prodromal and reactive elements.
4. Explore family history for serious mental illness.
5. Provide supportive therapy to alleviate fears and reduce feelings of alienation.
6. Explain the nature of the psychotic process, its biochemical component, and the confusing effect on rational thought.

and/or engaging in behavior that is harmful to self or others. (10)

8. Describe recent perceived severe stressors that may have precipitated acute psychotic break. (11, 12)

9. Take steps to change environment in such a way as to reduce the feelings of threat associated with it. (13)

10. Report diminishing or absence of hallucinations and/or delusions. (7, 8, 14, 15, 16)

11. Begin to show limited social functioning by responding appropriately to friendly encounters. (1, 5, 13, 14, 17)

12. Think more clearly as demonstrated by logical, coherent speech. (7, 8, 18, 19)

13. Verbalize an understanding of the underlying needs, conflicts, and emotions that support the irrational beliefs. (11, 14, 16, 20)

14. Family members increase their positive support of patient to reduce chances of acute exacerbation of psychotic episode. (21)

15. Family members to terminate double-bind messages that trigger patient's internal conflict. (22)

16. Family members share their feelings of guilt, frustration, and fear associated with patient's mental illness. (23)

7. Arrange for administration of appropriate psychotropic medications through a physician.

8. Monitor patient for medication compliance and redirect if patient is noncompliant.

9. Arrange for supervised living situation, if necessary.

10. Make arrangements for involuntary commitment to a inpatient psychiatric facility if the patient is unable to care for his/her basic needs or is harmful to self or others.

11. Probe causes for reactive psychosis.

12. Explore feelings surrounding stressors that triggered psychotic episodes.

13. Assist patient in reducing threat in the environment (e.g., finding a safer place to live, arrange for regular visits from caseworker, arrange for family members to call more frequently).

14. Assist in restructuring irrational beliefs by reviewing reality-based evidence and misinterpretation.

15. Encourage focus on the reality of the external world versus the patient's distorted fantasy.

16. Differentiate for patient the source of stimuli between self-generated messages and the reality of the external world.

17. Family members accept a referral to support group. (24)

18. Gradually return to premorbid level of functioning and accept responsibility of caring for own basic needs. (8, 14, 16, 18, 25)

—. _____
   _____

—. _____
   _____

—. _____
   _____

17. Reinforce socially and emotionally appropriate responses to others.

18. Gently confront illogical thoughts and speech to refocus disordered thinking.

19. Reinforce clarity and rationality of thought and speech.

20. Probe the underlying needs and feelings (e.g., inadequacy, rejection, anxiety, or guilt) that trigger irrational thought.

21. Arrange family therapy sessions to educate regarding patient's illness, treatment, and prognosis.

22. Assist family in avoiding double-bind messages that increase anxiety and psychotic symptoms in patient.

23. Encourage family members to share their feelings of frustration, guilt, fear, or depression surrounding patient's mental illness and behavior patterns.

24. Refer family members to a community-based support group designed for the family of psychotic patients.

25. Monitor patient's daily level of functioning—that is, reality orientation, personal hygiene, social interactions, and affect appropriateness—and give feedback that either redirects or reinforces patient's progress.

—. _____
    _____
—. _____
    _____
—. _____
    _____

DIAGNOSTIC SUGGESTIONS

Axis I:	297.1	Delusional Disorder
	298.8	Brief Psychotic Disorder
	295.xx	Schizophrenia
	295.30	Schizophrenia, Paranoid Type
	295.70	Schizoaffective Disorder
	295.40	Schizophreniform Disorder
	296.xx	Bipolar I Disorder
	296.89	Bipolar II Disorder
	296.xx	Major Depressive Disorder
	310.1	Personality Change Due to (Axis III Disorder)
	_____	_____
	_____	_____

SEXUAL ABUSE

BEHAVIORAL DEFINITIONS

1. Vague memories of inappropriate childhood sexual contact that can be corroborated by significant others.
2. Self-report of being sexually abused with clear, detailed memories.
3. Inability to recall years of childhood.
4. Extreme difficulty becoming intimate with others.
5. Inability to enjoy sexual contact with a desired partner.
6. Unexplainable feelings of anger, rage, or fear when coming into contact with a close family relative.
7. Pervasive pattern of promiscuity or the sexualization of relationships.

—. _____

_____

—. _____

_____

—. _____

_____

LONG-TERM GOALS

1. Resolve the issue of being sexually abused with an increased capacity for intimacy in relationships.
2. Begin the healing process from sexual abuse with resultant enjoyment of appropriate sexual contact.
3. Work successfully through the issues related to being sexually abused with consequent understanding and control of feelings.
4. Recognize and accept the sexual abuse without inappropriate sexualization of relationships.

5. Establish whether sexual abuse occurred.
6. Begin the process of moving away from being a victim of sexual abuse and toward becoming a survivor of sexual abuse.

—. _____
   _____
—. _____
   _____
—. _____
   _____

SHORT-TERM OBJECTIVES

THERAPEUTIC INTERVENTIONS

1. Tell the entire story of the abuse. (1, 2)

2. Identify the nature, frequency, and duration of the abuse. (1, 2, 3)

3. Identify and express the feelings connected to the abuse. (1, 4)

4. Identify a support system of key individuals who will be encouraging and helpful in aiding the process of resolving the issue. (5, 6)

5. Verbalize an increased knowledge of sexual abuse and its effect. (7, 8)

6. Demonstrate an increased ability to talk openly about the abuse, reflecting acceptance of the abuse. (1, 4, 9)

7. Decrease the secrecy in the family by informing key nonabusive members regarding the abuse. (10, 11, 12)

1. Actively build the level of trust with the patient in individual sessions through consistent eye contact, unconditional positive regard, and warm acceptance to help increase his/her ability to identify and express feelings.

2. Explore gently the sexual abuse experience without pressing early for unnecessary details.

3. Ask patient to draw a diagram of the house in which he/she was raised, complete with where everyone slept.

4. Explore, encourage, and support patient in verbally expressing and clarifying feelings associated with the abuse.

5. Help patient identify those individuals who would be supportive and encourage him/her to enlist their support.

8. Decrease feelings of shame by being able to verbally affirm self as not responsible for abuse. (6, 9, 13, 14, 22)

9. Clarify memories of the abuse. (3, 15, 16)

10. Express feelings to and about the perpetrator, including the impact the abuse has had both at the time of occurrence and currently. (10, 17, 18)

11. Verbalize the ways the sexual abuse has impacted his/her life. (7, 19, 20)

12. Describe how sex abuse experience is part of a family pattern of broken boundaries through physical contact or verbal suggestiveness. (21)

13. Read books that assist in overcoming shame. (22)

14. Decrease statements of being a victim while increasing statements that reflect personal empowerment. (13, 14, 23)

15. Verbally identify self as a survivor of sexual abuse. (7, 23, 24)

16. Identify the positive aspects for self of being able to forgive all those involved with the abuse. (3, 24, 25, 26)

17. Increase level of forgiveness of self, perpetrator, and others connected with the abuse. (26, 27)

6. Encourage patient to attend a support group for survivors of sexual abuse.

7. Assign patient to read *The Courage to Heal* (Bass and Davis), *Betrayal of Innocence* (Forward and Buck), or *Outgrowing the Pain* (Gil), and to process key concepts with therapist.

8. Assign and process a written exercise from *The Courage to Heal Workbook* (Davis).

9. Encourage patient to be open in talking of the abuse without shame or embarrassment as if he/she was responsible for the abuse.

10. Guide the patient in an empty chair conversation exercise with a key figure connected to the abuse (e.g., perpetrator, sibling, or parent) telling them of the sexual abuse and its effects.

11. Hold conjoint session where patient tells spouse of the abuse.

12. Facilitate family session with patient assisting and supporting him/her in revealing the abuse to parent(s).

13. Encourage, support, and assist the patient in identifying, expressing and processing any feelings of guilt related to feelings of physical pleasure, emotional fulfillment, or responsibility connected with the events.

18. Increase level of trust of others as shown by more socialization and greater intimacy tolerance. (6, 28, 29)

19. Report increased ability to accept and initiate appropriate physical contact with others. (30, 31)

__. _____
   _____

__. _____
   _____

__. _____
   _____

14. Confront and process with patient any statements that reflect responsibility for the abuse or indicate he/she is a victim. Then assist patient in feeling empowered by working through the issues and letting go of the abuse.

15. Refer or conduct hypnosis with patient to further uncover or to further clarify the nature and extent of the abuse.

16. Facilitate patient's recall of the details of the abuse by asking him/her to keep a journal and talk and think about the incident(s). Caution against embellishment based on book, video, or drama material, and be very careful not to lead the patient into only confirming therapist-held suspicions.

17. Assign patient to write an angry letter to the perpetrator and to process it with therapist.

18. Hold conjoint session where patient confronts the perpetrator of the abuse.

19. Develop with patient a symptom development line connected to the abuse.

20. Ask patient to make a list of the ways sexual abuse has impacted his/her life and to process the list with therapist.

21. Develop with patient a genogram and assist in illuminating key family patterns of broken boundaries related to sex and intimacy.

22. Assign patient to read sections in *Healing the Shame That Binds You* (Bradshaw), *Shame* (Kaufman), and *Facing Shame* (Fossum and Mason) and to process key concepts with therapist.

23. Ask patient to complete an exercise that identifies the positives and negatives of being a victim and the positives and negatives of being a survivor.

24. Assign patient to complete a cost-benefit exercise (see *Ten Days to Self-Esteem!* by Burns) on being a victim versus a survivor or on holding on versus forgiving, and process exercises with therapist.

25. Read and process the story from *Stories for the Third Ear* (Wallas) titled "The Seedling." (A story for a patient who has been abused as a child.)

26. Recommend that patient read *Forgive and Forget* (Smedes).

27. Assign patient to write a forgiveness letter and/or complete a forgiveness exercise (see *Forgiving* by Simon and Simon) and to process each with therapist.

28. Teach the patient the share-check method (i.e., sharing only a little of self and then checking to be sure that the shared data is treated respectfully, kindly, and confidentially; as proof of trustworthiness is verified, share more freely) of building trust in relationships.

29. Teach patient, using role-playing and modeling, how to establish reasonable personal boundaries that are neither too porous nor too restrictive.

30. Encourage patient to give and receive appropriate touches, helping him/her define what is appropriate.

31. Ask patient to practice one or two times a week initiating touching or a touching activity (i.e., giving a back rub to spouse, receiving a professional massage, hugging a friend, etc.).

__. _____

_____

__. _____

_____

__. _____

_____

DIAGNOSTIC SUGGESTIONS

Axis I:
303.90	Alcohol Dependence	
304.80	Polysubstance Dependence	
300.4	Dysthymic Disorder	
296.xx	Major Depressive Disorder	
300.02	Generalized Anxiety Disorder	
300.14	Dissociative Identity Disorder	
300.15	Dissociative Disorder NOS	
V61.21	Sexual Abuse of Child (995.5, Victim)	
V61.1	Sexual Abuse of Adult (995.81, Victim)	
_____	_____	
_____	_____	

Axis II:
301.82	Avoidant Personality Disorder	
301.6	Dependent Personality Disorder	
_____	_____	
_____	_____	

SLEEP DISTURBANCE

BEHAVIORAL DEFINITIONS

1. Difficulty getting to or maintaining sleep.
2. Sleeping adequately but not feeling refreshed or rested after waking.
3. Predominant daytime sleepiness or falling asleep too easily during daytime.
4. Insomnia or hypersomnia complaints due to a reversal of the sleep-wake schedule normal for the patient's environment.
5. Distress resulting from repeated awakening with detailed recall of extremely frightening dreams involving threats to self.
6. Abrupt awakening with a panicky scream followed by intense anxiety and autonomic arousal, no detailed dream recall, and confusion or disorientation.
7. Repeated incidents of sleepwalking accompanied by amnesia for the episode.

—. _____
_____

—. _____
_____

—. _____
_____

LONG-TERM GOALS

1. Restore restful sleep pattern.
2. Feel refreshed and energetic during wakeful hours.
3. Terminate anxiety-producing dreams that cause awakening.

4. End abrupt awakening in terror and return to peaceful, restful sleep pattern.
5. Restore restful sleep with reduction of sleepwalking incidents.

—. _____
_____

—. _____
_____

—. _____
_____

SHORT-TERM OBJECTIVES

1. Describe details of sleep pattern and its history. (1, 2)
2. Keep a journal of daily stressors and associated sleep pattern. (1, 2)
3. Share history of substance abuse or medication use. (3)
4. Keep physician appointment to assess organic contributions to sleep disorder and the need for psychotropic medications. (4, 17)
5. Verbalize depressive feelings and share possible causes. (2, 3, 5)
6. Discuss experiences of emotional traumas that continue to disturb sleep. (6)
7. Describe disturbing dreams by keeping a dream journal. (7, 8)
8. Discuss fears regarding relinquishing control. (8)

THERAPEUTIC INTERVENTIONS

1. Assess the exact nature of sleep pattern, including bedtime routine, activity level while awake, nutritional habits, napping practice, actual sleep time, rhythm of time for being awake versus sleeping, and so on.
2. Assign patient to keep a journal of daily stressors and nightly sleep patterns.
3. Assess contribution of medication or substance abuse to sleep disorder.
4. Refer to physician to rule out physical and pharmacological causes for sleep disturbance and evaluate for psychotropic medications.
5. Assess role of depression as cause of sleep disturbance.
6. Explore recent traumatic events that interfere with sleep.

9. Disclose fears of death that may contribute to sleep disturbance. (8, 9)

10. Identify current stressors that may be interfering with sleep. (2, 6, 10)

11. Verbalize a plan to deal with stressors proactively. (10, 11)

12. Share childhood traumatic experiences associated with sleep experience. (7, 12)

13. Reveal sexual abuse incidents that continue to be disturbing. (7, 13)

14. Follow sleep induction schedule of events. (14)

15. Practice deep muscle relaxation exercises. (15, 16)

16. Utilize biofeedback training to deepen relaxation skill. (15, 16)

17. Take antidepressant medication daily for 3 weeks to assess effect on sleep. (4, 17, 18)

18. Cooperate with sleep clinic referral and evaluation. (19)

—. _____
_____

—. _____
_____

—. _____
_____

7. Probe nature of disturbing dreams and relationship to life stress. Assign patient to keep a dream journal.

8. Probe fears related to letting go of control.

9. Probe fear of death that may contribute to sleep disturbance.

10. Identify the current life circumstances that are causing anxiety that may be interfering with sleep.

11. Assist patient in formulating a plan to modify life situation to reduce stress and anxiety.

12. Explore traumas of childhood that surround the sleep experience.

13. Explore possible sexual abuse that has not been revealed.

14. Assign adherence to a strict sleep induction routine: daily exercise, low stimulation prior to sleep, relaxation training, bland diet, warm bath, reading a book, and so forth.

15. Train in deep muscle relaxation and deep breathing exercises with and without audiotape instruction.

16. Administer electromyographic (EMG) biofeedback to reinforce successful relaxation response.

17. Arrange for antidepressant medication to enhance restful sleep.

18. Monitor patient for medication compliance and effectiveness.

19. Refer to sleep clinic for assessment of sleep apnea or other physiological factors.

—. _____
_____

—. _____
_____

—. _____
_____

DIAGNOSTIC SUGGESTIONS

Axis I: 307.42 Primary Insomnia
307.44 Primary Hypersomnia
307.45 Circadian Rhythm Sleep Disorder
307.47 Nightmare Disorder
307.46 Sleep Terror Disorder
307.46 Sleepwalking Disorder
309.81 Posttraumatic Stress Disorder
296.xx Major Depressive Disorder
300.4 Dysthymic Disorder

_____   _____
_____   _____

SOCIAL DISCOMFORT

BEHAVIORAL DEFINITIONS

1. Overall pattern of social anxiety, shyness, or timidity that presents itself in most social situations.
2. Hypersensitivity to the criticism or disapproval of others.
3. No close friends or confidants outside of first-degree relatives.
4. Avoidance of situations that require a degree of interpersonal contact.
5. Reluctant involvement in social situations out of fear of saying or doing something foolish or of becoming emotional in front of others.
6. Abuse of alcohol or chemicals to help ease the anxiety of becoming involved in social situations.
7. Isolation or involvement in solitary activities during most waking hours.
8. Increased heart rate, sweating, dry mouth, muscle tension, and shakiness in most social situations.

__. _____
   _____
__. _____
   _____
__. _____
   _____

LONG-TERM GOALS

1. Interact socially without excessive fear or anxiety.
2. Develop the essential social skills that will enhance the quality of relationship life.

214

3. Develop the ability to form relationships that will enhance recovery support system.
4. Reach a personal balance between solitary time and interpersonal interaction with others.
5. Terminate use of alcohol or chemicals to relieve social anxiety and learn constructive coping behaviors.

__. _____
   _____
__. _____
   _____
__. _____
   _____

SHORT-TERM OBJECTIVES

1. Identify and clarify nature of fears connected to associating with others. (1, 2, 3)

2. Identify sources of low self-esteem and initiate one social contact per day for increasing lengths of time. (1, 4)

3. Identify how shame affects relating with others. (2, 4)

4. Recall past positive experiences of being involved in social activities and/or relating one-on-one with others. (5)

5. Identify negative self-talk that fosters social anxiety. (6, 18, 19)

6. Develop a positive self-talk dialogue that will help overcome fear of interacting with others. (7)

THERAPEUTIC INTERVENTIONS

1. Assist patient in identifying fears tied to relating with others.

2. Probe childhood experiences of criticism, abandonment, or abuse that would foster low self-esteem and shame.

3. Explore childhood and adolescent experiences of rejection and neglect that would foster fear of rejection.

4. Assign client to read the books *Healing the Shame That Binds You* (Bradshaw) and *Facing Shame* (Fossum and Mason), and process key ideas.

5. Ask patient to list and process positive experiences from social activities.

7. Initiate one social contact per day with a familiar person for increasing lengths of time. (8, 9)

8. Verbally report positive outcomes of participation in social and support groups. (9, 10, 11, 12)

9. Participate verbally in a meaningful way in group experiences. (10, 11, 13, 14)

10. Initiate a social contact with a stranger. (12, 15)

11. Identify and implement again successful social skills from the past. (5, 16)

12. Identify ways he/she is like other people and therefore acceptable to others. (17, 18, 19, 20)

13. Increase feelings and statements of self acceptance. (19, 21, 22)

14. Implement assertiveness skills. (13, 14, 23)

15. Verbally describe the defense mechanisms used to avoid close relationships. (22, 24)

16. Verbally report and demonstrate a renewed sense of trust in others. (12, 20, 21, 25)

17. Develop a written plan that divides nonworkdays between social and solitary activities. (12, 19, 26)

6. Assist patient in identifying distorted automatic thoughts associated with anxiety over social interaction.

7. Assist patient in developing positive self-talk that will aid in overcoming fear of relating with others or participating in social activities.

8. Assign patient to initiate one conversation daily, increasing time from 1 minute to 5 minutes per interaction, and report results to therapist.

9. Monitor, encourage, redirect, and give positive feedback to patient as necessary relating to his/her interaction with others.

10. Ask patient to attend and participate in available social and recreational activities within treatment program or the community.

11. Refer patient to self-help group (i.e., AA, NA, Emotions Anonymous, or Recovery, Inc.) and process the experience with therapist.

12. Encourage and support patient in his/her effort to initiate and build social relationships.

13. Assign patient to self-disclose two times in each group therapy session.

14. Refer patient to attend a communication improvement seminar or a Dale Carnegie course.

___. _____

_____

___. _____

_____

___. _____

_____

15. Facilitate a role-play with patient around initiating a conversation with another person for the first time. Process the experience.

16. Utilize a brief solution-oriented approach to identify a time where patient socialized with enjoyment and little anxiety, then create a situation that involves the same elements and have patient use this social coping skill consistently in following weeks. Monitor and adjust as necessary.

17. Read either "Jean and Jane" or "The Wallflower" from *Friedman's Fables* (Friedman) to the patient, then use the accompanying questions to process the fable with him/her.

18. Ask patient to read the "Social Anxiety" section in *The Feeling Good Handbook* (Burns) and process key ideas with therapist.

19. Assign patient to complete and process exercises on social anxiety and thought distortion in *Ten Days to Self Esteem!* (Burns).

20. Assist patient in recognizing how he/she is like or similar to others.

21. Assign patient to read *Born To Win* (James and Jongeward), *Pulling Your Own Strings* (Dyer), or *I'm OK You're OK* (Harris and Harris) to help patient see self

more clearly and in a different, more hopeful light.

22. Utilize a transactional analysis (TA) approach to undercover and identify patient's beliefs and fears. Then use the TA approach to alter beliefs and actions.

23. Train patient in assertiveness skills or refer to an assertiveness-training class.

24. Assist patient in identifying defense mechanisms that keep others at a distance and in identifying ways to keep defensiveness at a minimum.

25. Reinforce patient's statements that reflect increased trust that others will be and are accepting of self.

26. Ask patient to develop a daily plan for nonworking hours that contains both social and solitary activities. Review plan and give feedback.

__. _____

_____

__. _____

_____

__. _____

_____

DIAGNOSTIC SUGGESTIONS

Axis I:	300.23	Social Phobia
	300.4	Dysthymic Disorder
	296.xx	Major Depressive Disorder
	300.21	Panic Disorder with Agoraphobia
	309.81	Posttraumatic Stress Disorder
	_____	_____
	_____	_____
Axis II:	301.82	Avoidant Personality Disorder
	301.20	Schizoid Personality Disorder
	301.0	Paranoid Personality Disorder
	301.22	Schizotypal Personality Disorder
	_____	_____
	_____	_____

SOMATIZATION

BEHAVIORAL DEFINITIONS

1. Preoccupation with some imagined defect in appearance or excessive concern regarding a small physical abnormality.
2. A physical malady caused by a psychosocial stressor triggering a psychological conflict.
3. Preoccupation with the fear of having a serious physical disease without any medical basis for concern.
4. A multitude of physical complaints that have no organic foundation and have caused the patient to change his/her life (e.g., seeing doctors often, taking prescriptions, and withdrawing from responsibilities).
5. Preoccupation with chronic pain grossly beyond what is expected for a physical malady or in spite of no known organic cause.
6. One or more physical complaints (usually vague) that have no known organic basis, or the complaining and impairment in life functioning are in excess of what is expected.
7. Preoccupation with pain in one or more anatomical sites with both psychological factors and a medical condition as a basis for the pain.

__. _____
   _____
__. _____
   _____
__. _____
   _____

LONG-TERM GOALS

1. Reduce frequency of physical complaints and improve the level of independent functioning.
2. Reduce verbalizations focusing on pain while increasing productive activities.
3. Accept body appearance as normal even with insignificant flaws.
4. Accept self as relatively healthy with no known medical illness.
5. Improve physical functioning due to development of adequate coping mechanisms for stress management.

—. _____

_____

—. _____

_____

—. _____

_____

SHORT-TERM OBJECTIVES

1. Verbalize negative feelings regarding body and discuss self-prediction of catastrophized consequences of perceived body abnormality. (1, 2, 3)
2. Discuss causes for emotional stress in life that underlie the focus on physical complaints. (1, 3)
3. Verbalize the secondary gain that results from physical complaints. (4)
4. Verbalize an understanding of a relationship between emotional conflict and physical complaints. (5)
5. Identify causes for anger. (6)

THERAPEUTIC INTERVENTIONS

1. Listen to patient's initial complaints without rejection or confrontation.
2. Refocus patient's discussion from physical complaints to emotional conflicts and expression of feelings.
3. Explore sources of emotional pain: feelings of fear, inadequacy, rejection, or abuse.
4. Assist patient in developing insight into the secondary gain received from physical illness, complaints, and the like.
5. Assist patient in acceptance of connection between physical focus and avoidance of facing emotional conflicts.

6. Express angry feelings assertively and directly. (7, 8, 9)

7. List pleasurable and constructive activities that can serve as a diversion from self-preoccupation. (10)

8. Increase social and productive activities rather than being preoccupied with self and physical complaints. (10, 11)

9. Identify family patterns that exist around exaggerated focus on physical maladies. (12)

10. Identify causes for feelings of low self-esteem and inadequacy based in early family history. (13)

11. Identify the connection between negative body image and general low self-esteem. (13, 14)

12. Verbalize acceptance of body as normal in function and appearance. (15, 16)

13. Implement the use of relaxation skills to reduce tension in response to stress. (17)

14. Increase daily exercise regimen to reduce tension and increase a sense of confidence in own body. (18)

15. Report on instances of taking active control over environmental events versus passively reacting like a victim. (19)

6. Explore causes for anger.

7. Using role-playing and behavioral rehearsal, teach assertive, respectful expression of angry feelings.

8. Train in assertiveness or refer to an assertiveness-training class.

9. Reinforce assertiveness as means of attaining healthy need satisfaction in contrast to whining helplessness.

10. Assign patient to develop a list of pleasurable activities that can serve as rewards and diversions from bodily focus.

11. Assign diversion activities that take focus off self and redirect toward hobby, social activities, assisting others, completing projects, or returning to work.

12. Explore family history of modeling and reinforcement of physical complaints.

13. Probe causes for low self-esteem and fears of inadequacy in childhood experiences.

14. Teach the patient the connection between low self-esteem and preoccupation with body image.

15. Give positive feedback when patient is symptom-free and accepting of body as normal.

16. Make worries into metaphor of "making sure he/she stays healthy." Then

16. Set aside a specific, limited time each day to focus on, talk about, and journalize details of physical complaints. (20)
17. Implement a self-punishment technique to reduce the focus on physical symptoms. (21)
18. List coping behaviors that will be implemented when physical symptoms appear. (22)
19. Poll family and friends regarding their concern about patient's physical complaints. (23)
20. Decrease physical complaints, doctor visits, and reliance on medication while increasing verbal assessment of self as able to function normally and productively. (15, 19, 24)
21. Engage in normal responsibilities vocationally and socially without complaints or withdrawal into avoidance using physical problem as excuse. (15, 19, 24, 25)
22. Accept referral to a pain clinic to learn pain management techniques. (26)

__. _____
   _____
__. _____
   _____
__. _____
   _____

issue a prescription for increased exercise, sex, or joy, along with a plan of how to implement.
17. Train patient in relaxation techniques using biofeedback, deep breathing, and positive imagery techniques.
18. Assign patient to a daily exercise routine.
19. Empower patient to take control of his/her environment rather than continue helplessness, frustration, anger and "poor me."
20. Structure specific times each day for the patient to think about, talk about, and write down his/her physical problems. Outside of those times patient will not focus on physical condition. Monitor and process intervention's effectiveness.
21. Create an ordeal for patient to do each time the symptom (physical complaint) occurs. (An ordeal is a specific task which is necessary in patient's daily life but one he/she finds unpleasant.) Convince the patient of the effectiveness of this prescription and monitor for compliance and results.
22. Talk in session with patient about predicting the next attack or physical issue and then plan how patient will handle it when it comes.

23. Assign to the patient the ritual of polling spouse, friends, neighbors, pastors, and so on about how concerned they feel he/she should be, how concerned they would be, and what they would recommend he/she do each time a physical complaint/concern occurs. Report results to therapist.

24. Challenge patient to endure pain and carry on with responsibilities so as to build self-esteem and a sense of contribution.

25. Discuss the destructive social impact on friends and family of consistent complaintive verbalization or negative body focus.

26. Refer patient to a pain clinic.

__. _____
   _____

__. _____
   _____

__. _____
   _____

DIAGNOSTIC SUGGESTIONS

Axis I:

300.7	Body Dysmorphic Disorder
300.11	Conversion Disorder
300.7	Hypochondriasis
300.81	Somatization Disorder
307.80	Pain Disorder Associated with Psychological Factors
307.89	Pain Disorder Associated with Both Psychological Factors and an Axis III Disorder
300.81	Undifferentiated Somatoform Disorder
300.4	Dysthymic Disorder
_____	_____
_____	_____

SPIRITUAL CONFUSION

BEHAVIORAL DEFINITIONS

1. Verbalization of a desire for a closer relationship to a higher power.
2. Feelings and attitudes about higher power that are characterized by fear, anger, and distrust.
3. Verbalizes a feeling of emptiness in his/her life, as if something were missing.
4. Negative, bleak outlook on life and others.
5. Upbringing contained no religious education or training, and patient now feels a need to have a higher power in his/her life but does not know where or how to begin.
6. Anger, hurt, and so on from religious upbringing has left patient paralyzed and unable to connect with a higher power.
7. A struggle with understanding and accepting Alcoholics Anonymous (AA) Steps 2 and 3 and difficulty in believing in a higher power.

—. _____
_____
—. _____
_____
—. _____
_____

LONG-TERM GOALS

1. Clarify spiritual concepts and instill a freedom to approach a higher power as a resource for support.
2. Increase belief in and development of a relationship with a higher power.

3. Begin a faith in a higher power and incorporate it into a support system.
4. Resolve issues that have prevented faith or belief from developing and growing.

—. _____

—. _____

—. _____

SHORT-TERM OBJECTIVES

1. Summarize the highlights of the spiritual quest or journey to this date. (1)

2. Describe beliefs around the idea of a higher power. (2, 3)

3. Describe early life training in spiritual concepts and identify its impact on current belief. (4)

4. Verbalize an increase of knowledge and understanding of a concept of a higher power. (5, 6)

5. Identify and verbalize feelings related to a higher power. (2, 4, 7)

6. Describe negative life experiences associated with religious faith. (8)

7. Identify specific blocks to believing in a higher power. (8, 9)

THERAPEUTIC INTERVENTIONS

1. Ask patient to write story of his/her spiritual quest/journey and process it with therapist.

2. Assist in processing and clarifying ideas and feelings regarding a higher power.

3. Assign patient to list all beliefs related to a higher power and then process the beliefs.

4. Review early life experiences surrounding belief in a higher power.

5. Ask patient to talk with a chaplain, pastor, rabbi, or priest regarding spiritual struggles, issues, or questions he/she has and record their feedback.

6. Assign patient to read *God: A Biography* (Miles) or *The History of God* (Armstrong) to build knowledge and a concept of a higher power.

8. Read books that detail the experience of others who have had spiritual struggles. (10)

9. Implement daily attempts to be in contact with higher power. (11, 12, 13)

10. Identify the difference between religion and faith. (10, 14)

11. Replace the concept of a higher power as harsh and judgmental with a belief in a higher power as forgiving and loving. (10, 15)

12. Compare beliefs in higher power with attitudes and feelings toward earthly father. (16)

13. Verbalize separation of beliefs and feelings toward earthly father from those toward a higher power. (17)

14. Agree to try to separate negative experiences with religious people from current spiritual evaluation. (8, 18)

15. Verbalize acceptance of forgiveness from a higher power. (19, 20)

16. Ask a respected person who has apparent spiritual depth to serve as a mentor. (21)

17. Attend groups dedicated to enriching spirituality. (22, 23)

18. Read books that focus on communicating with a higher power. (24)

7. Explore emotional components (e.g., fear, rejection, peace, acceptance, abandonment, etc.) of patient's reaction to a higher power.

8. Explore religious distortions and judgmentalism that patient was subjected to by others.

9. Assist patient in identifying specific issues or blocks that prevent the development of his/her spirituality.

10. Encourage patient to read books dealing with conversion experiences such as *Surprised by Joy* (Lewis), *Confessions of St. Augustine* (Augustine), *The Seven Storey Mountain* (Merton), or *Soul On Fire* (Cleaver).

11. Recommend implementation of daily meditations and/or prayer. Process the experience.

12. Assign patient to write a daily note to his/her power.

13. Assist patient in developing and encourage implementing a daily devotional time or other rituals that will foster his/her spiritual growth.

14. Educate patient on the difference between religion and spirituality.

15. Emphasize that the higher power is characterized by love and gracious forgiveness for anyone with remorse and who seeks forgiveness.

—. _____
   _____
—. _____
   _____
—. _____
   _____

16. Assist patient in comparing beliefs and feelings about earthly father with those about a higher power.

17. Urge separating the feelings and beliefs regarding the earthly father from those toward a higher power to allow for spiritual growth and maturity.

18. Assist in evaluating religious tenets separated from painful emotional experience with religious people in patient's past.

19. Ask patient to read the books *Serenity* (Helmfelt and Fowler)—all readings related to AA Steps 2 and 3; *The Road Less Traveled* (Peck); and *Search for Serenity* (Presnall).

20. Explore feelings of shame and guilt that led to feeling unworthy to higher power and others.

21. Help patient find a spiritual mentor to guide his/her development.

22. Make patient aware of opportunities such as Bible studies, study groups, fellowship groups, and so on, and process the experiences he/she decides to pursue.

23. Suggest patient attend a spiritual retreat such as De Colores or Course in Miracles and report to therapist what the experience was like for him/her and what was gained from the experience.

24. Ask patient to read *Clois-tered Walk* (Norris), *Hymns to an Unknown God* (Keen), and *The Care of the Soul* (Moore) to expand ways of cultivating his/her spirituality.

—. _____

   _____

—. _____

   _____

—. _____

   _____

DIAGNOSTIC SUGGESTIONS

Axis I: 300.4   Dysthymic Disorder
             311   Depressive Disorder NOS
             300.00   Anxiety Disorder NOS
             296.xx   Major Depressive Disorder

             _____   _____

             _____   _____

SUICIDAL IDEATION

BEHAVIORAL DEFINITIONS

1. Recurrent thoughts of or preoccupation with death.
2. Recurrent or ongoing suicidal ideation without any plans.
3. Ongoing suicidal ideation with a specific plan.
4. Recent suicide attempt.
5. History of suicide attempts that required professional or family/ friend intervention on some level (i.e., inpatient, safe house, out- patient, or supervision).
6. Positive family history of depression and/or a preoccupation with suicidal thoughts.
7. A bleak, hopeless attitude regarding life coupled with recent life events that support this (i.e., divorce, death of a friend or family member, or loss of job).
8. Social withdrawal, lethargy, and apathy coupled with expressions of wanting to die.
9. Sudden change from being depressed to upbeat and at peace while actions indicate patient is "putting his/her house in order" and there has been no genuine resolution of conflict issues.

—. _____

_____

—. _____

_____

—. _____

_____

LONG-TERM GOALS

1. Alleviate the suicidal impulses/ideation and return to the highest level of previous daily functioning.
2. Stabilize the suicidal crisis.
3. Placement in an appropriate level of care to safely address the suicidal crisis.
4. Reestablish a sense of hope for self and the future.
5. Cease the perilous lifestyle and resolve the emotional conflicts that underlie the suicidal pattern.

—. _____
_____
—. _____
_____
—. _____
_____

SHORT-TERM OBJECTIVES

1. State the strength of the suicidal feelings, the frequency of the thoughts, and the detail of the plans. (1, 2, 3, 4)
2. Verbalize a promise (as part of a suicide-prevention contract) to contact the therapist or some other emergency helpline if a serious urge toward self-harm arises. (5, 6, 7, 8)
3. Commit to and follow all the stipulations in the suicide contract. (5, 6, 7, 8)
4. Follow through with all of the professional recommendations for the suicidal crisis. (5, 8, 9)

THERAPEUTIC INTERVENTIONS

1. Assess suicidal ideation, taking into account extent of ideation, the presence of a primary and back-up plan, past attempts, and family history.
2. Assess and monitor suicidal potential on an ongoing basis.
3. Notify family and significant others of the suicidal ideation. Ask them to form a 24-hour suicide watch until the crisis subsides.
4. Arrange for patient to take Minnesota Multiphasic Personality Inventory (MMPI), Beck Depression Inventory (BDI), or Modified Scale for

5. Increase the safety of the home by removing firearms or other lethal weapons from easy access. (3, 9)

6. Report suicidal impulses to a designated significant other or helping professional. (2, 3, 6, 8, 10)

7. Cooperate with hospitalization if the suicidal urge becomes uncontrollable. (2, 5, 11)

8. Identify life factors that preceded the suicidal ideation. (12, 13, 19)

9. Increase communication with significant others, resulting in a feeling of understanding, empathy, and being attended to. (14, 15, 16)

10. Identify feelings of sadness, anger, and hopelessness related to a conflicted relationship with significant others. (14, 15, 16)

11. Significant others verbalize an understanding of the patient's feelings of alienation and hopelessness. (14, 16)

12. Cooperate with a referral to a physician for an evaluation for antidepressant medication. (17)

13. Take medications as prescribed and report all side effects. (2, 17, 18)

14. Express, with appropriate affect, feelings that underlie suicidal ideation. (12, 13, 19)

Suicide Ideation (MSSI) and evaluate results for degree of depression and suicide risk.

5. Elicit a promise from patient that he/she will initiate contact with the therapist or a helpline if the suicidal urge becomes strong and before any self-injurious behavior.

6. Provide patient with an emergency helpline telephone number that is available 24 hours a day.

7. Make a contract with patient, identifying what he/she will and won't do when experiencing suicidal thoughts or impulses.

8. Offer to be available to patient through telephone contact if a life-threatening urge develops.

9. Encourage significant others to remove firearms or other lethal weapons from patient's easy access.

10. Encourage patient to be open and honest regarding suicidal urges, reassuring regularly of caring concern by therapist and significant others.

11. Arrange for hospitalization when patient is judged to be uncontrollably harmful to self.

12. Explore sources of emotional pain and hopelessness.

15. Disclose the distress caused by broken romantic or social friendships that has led to feelings of abject loneliness and rejection. (12, 13, 19, 20)

16. Identify how his/her previous attempts to solve interpersonal problems have failed, resulting in helplessness. (19, 20, 21)

17. Reestablish a consistent eating and sleeping pattern. (2, 18, 22)

18. Report a decrease in the frequency and intensity of the suicidal ideation. (2, 4, 13, 23)

19. Verbally report and demonstrate an increased sense of hope for self (2, 23, 24)

20. Report no longer feeling the impulse to take own life. (2, 23, 24)

21. Identify the positive aspects, relationships, and achievements in his/her life. (24, 25)

22. Identify negative thinking patterns that mediate feelings of hopelessness and helplessness. (26, 27)

23. Verbalize more positive cognitive processing patterns that maintain a realistic and hopeful perspective. (27, 28, 29)

24. Develop and implement a penitence ritual in which one expresses grief for victims and absolves self of

13. Encourage patient to express feelings related to suicidal ideation in order to clarify them and increase insight as to the causes.

14. Meet with significant others to assess their understanding of the causes for patient's distress.

15. Probe patient's feelings of despair related to his/her family relationships.

16. Hold family therapy sessions to promote communication of the patient's feelings of sadness, hurt, and anger.

17. Assess the need for antidepressant medication and arrange for a prescription, if necessary.

18. Monitor patient for effect of and compliance with prescribed medication. Confer with prescribing physician on a regular basis.

19. Assist patient in becoming aware of life factors that were significant precursors to the beginning of his/her suicidal ideation.

20. Encourage patient to share feelings of grief related to broken close relationships.

21. Review with patient previous problem-solving attempts and discuss new alternatives that are available.

22. Encourage normal eating and sleeping patterns and monitor compliance.

guilt for surviving an incident fatal to others. (30)

25. Verbalize a feeling of support that results from spiritual faith. (31, 32)

—. _____
   _____

—. _____
   _____

—. _____
   _____

23. Assist patient in developing coping strategies for suicidal ideation (e.g., more physical exercise, less internal focus, increased social involvement, and more expression of feelings).

24. Assist patient in finding positive, hopeful things in his/her life at the present time.

25. Review with patient the success he/she has had and the sources of love and concern that exist in his/her life. Ask patient to write a list of positive aspects of his/her life.

26. Assist patient in developing an awareness of the cognitive messages that reinforce hopelessness and helplessness.

27. Identify and confront catastrophizing tendencies in patient's cognitive processing, allowing for a more realistic perspective of hope in the face of pain.

28. Train patient in revising core schemes using cognitive restructuring techniques.

29. Require patient to keep a daily record of self-defeating thoughts (thoughts of hopelessness, helplessness, worthlessness, catastrophizing, negatively predicting the future, etc.), challenge each thought for accuracy, then replace each dysfunctional thought with one that

is positive and self-enhancing.

30. Develop a penitence ritual for patient with suicidal ideation connected with being a survivor and implement it with him/her.

31. Explore patient's spiritual belief system as to it being a source of acceptance and peace.

32. Arrange for patient's spiritual leader to meet with and support patient.

__. _____
_____

__. _____
_____

__. _____
_____

DIAGNOSTIC SUGGESTIONS

Axis I: 296.xx   Bipolar I Disorder
300.4   Dysthymic Disorder
296.2x   Major Depressive Disorder, Single Episode
296.3x   Major Depressive Disorder, Recurrent
296.89   Bipolar II Disorder

_____   _____
_____   _____

Axis II: 301.83   Borderline Personality Disorder

_____   _____
_____   _____

TYPE A BEHAVIOR

BEHAVIORAL DEFINITIONS

1. A pattern of pressuring self and others to accomplish more because there is never enough time.
2. A spirit of intense competition in all activities.
3. Intense compulsion to win at all costs regardless of the activity or co-competitor.
4. Inclination to dominate all social or business situations, being too direct and overbearing.
5. Propensity to become irritated by the action of others who do not conform to patient's sense of propriety or correctness.
6. A state of perpetual impatience with any waiting, delays, or interruptions.
7. Difficulty in sitting and quietly relaxing or reflecting.
8. Psychomotor facial signs of intensity and pressure such as muscle tension, scowling, glaring, or tics.
9. Psychomotor voice signs such as irritatingly forceful speech or laughter, rapid and intense speech, and frequent use of obscenities.

__. _____
   _____

__. _____
   _____

__. _____
   _____

LONG-TERM GOALS

1. Formulate and implement a new life attitudinal pattern that allows for a more relaxed pattern of living.
2. Reach a balance between work/competitive and social/noncompetitive time in daily life.
3. Achieve an overall decrease in pressured, driven behaviors.
4. Develop social and recreational activities as a routine part of life.
5. Alleviate sense of time urgency, free-floating anxiety, and self-destructive behaviors.

__. _____

_____

_____

__. _____

_____

__. _____

_____

SHORT-TERM OBJECTIVES

1. Describe the pattern of pressured, driven living. (1, 2)
2. Comply with psychological assessment. (3, 4)
3. Identify family of origin dynamics that foster a driven lifestyle. (5)
4. Identify specifically the beliefs that support driven, overachieving behavior. (5, 6, 7)
5. Practice deep muscle relaxation to relieve tension and slow pace of life. (8)
6. Decrease number of hours worked daily and taking work home. (6, 9)

THERAPEUTIC INTERVENTIONS

1. Ask patient to give examples of pressured lifestyle.
2. Assist patient to see self as others do.
3. Administer or refer patient for personality testing.
4. Review and process results of testing with patient.
5. Probe family of origin history for role models of or parental pressure for high achievement and compulsive drive.
6. Assign patient to read the books *Positive Addiction* (Glasser) and *Overdoing It* (Robinson) and to select key ideas to discuss with therapist.

7. Increase daily time involved in relaxing activities. (9, 10, 11)

8. Identify values that provide motivation for overemphasis on accomplishment, achievement, and success. (12)

9. Verbalize a desire to reprioritize values toward less self-focus, more inner and other orientation. (12, 13)

10. Develop pattern of doing one task at a time with less emphasis on pressure to complete it quickly. (14)

11. Balance time spent on daily activities of work and leisure. (9, 10, 11, 15, 16)

12. Verbalize a recognition of hostility toward and impatience with others. (17, 18, 19, 20)

13. Identify the sources of hostility. (18, 19, 20)

14. Verbalize the distinction between respectful assertiveness and insensitive directness or verbal aggression that is controlling. (21, 22)

15. Identify pattern of trying unsuccessfully to please a parent figure since childhood. (5, 23)

16. Increase active listening to others in conversation. (22, 24)

17. Identify distorted automatic thoughts that motivate pressured living. (25)

7. Ask patient to make a list of his/her beliefs about self-worth and the worth of others. Process it with therapist.

8. Train patient in deep muscle relaxation and breathing exercises to slow pace of life.

9. Review patient's pattern of hours spent working (at home and office) and recommend a significant reduction.

10. Assign patient to do one noncompetitive, recreational activity each day for a week and to process this experience with therapist.

11. Ask patient to try one area of interest outside of his/her vocation that he/she will do two times weekly for one month.

12. Explore and clarify patient's value system and assist in developing new priorities on the importance of relationships, recreation, spiritual growth, relfection time, giving to others, and so on.

13. Ask patient to read biographies or autobiographies of people (St. Augustine, Thomas Merton, Albert Schweitzer, C. S. Lewis, etc.) and process the key beliefs they lived by with therapist.

14. Encourage and reinforce focusing on one activity at a time without urgency.

18. Verbalize self-talk that promotes a slower pace, greater self-acceptance, and sensitivity to others. (22, 26)

19. Demonstrate decreased impatience with others by talking of appreciating and understanding the good qualities of others. (13, 27, 28)

20. Increase interest in the lives of others as evidenced by listening to others talk of their life experiences, and by engaging in one act of kindness per day. (29, 30, 31)

21. Identify the positive aspects of employing understanding, compassion, kindness, and forgiveness in dealing with others. (29, 30)

22. Demonstrate increased ability to give love by being more affectionate physically and verbally. (30, 32)

23. Develop a daily routine that reflects a balance between the quest for achievement and appreciation of aesthetic things. (16, 29, 31, 32)

—. _____
   _____

—. _____
   _____

—. _____
   _____

15. Assign patient to watch comedy movies and identify the positive aspects of them with therapist.

16. Reinforce all patient changes that reflect a greater sense of life balance.

17. Explore patterns of intolerant, impatient interaction with others.

18. Assist patient in identifying his/her critical beliefs about other people and connecting them to behavior patterns in daily life.

19. Reflect patient's hostility and assist in identifying its source.

20. Give patient an Ericksonian assignment—that is, at a certain time drive ___ miles exactly, stop, pull over, and think about ___ for ___ minutes, then return and process assignment with therapist.

21. Train patient in assertiveness to learn to avoid aggression and trampling on rights of others.

22. Confront and reframe patient's actions or verbalizations when he/she is self-centered or reflects a lack of feeling for others. Use role-playing and role reversal exercises to increase empathy for others' feelings.

23. Probe family of origin for history of being pressured to achieve but never suc-

ceeding at satisfying a parent figure.

24. Assign patient to talk to an
associate or child, focusing
on listening to the other
person and learning several
key things about that
person.

25. Assist patient in identifying
distorted automatic
thoughts that lead to feeling pressured to achieve.

26. Train patient in self-talk
that will assist in altering
beliefs that foster the compulsive behaviors.

27. Assign patient and family
to attend an experiential
weekend that promotes self-
awareness (e.g., high-low
ropes course or cooperative
tasks) and process experience afterwards with
therapist.

28. Assign patient to go with
a group on a wilderness
camping and canoeing trip,
on a work camp project, or
with the Red Cross as a
disaster worker.

29. Encourage patient to volunteer for a nonprofit social
agency, school, or the like
for one year doing direct
work with people (i.e., serv-
ing food at a soup kitchen or
tutoring an inner-city child)
and process the positive
consequences.

30. Encourage and monitor patient in doing one random,

spontaneous act of kindness on a daily basis and explore the positive results.

31. Assign patient to read the book *The Road Less Traveled* (Peck) and to process key ideas with therapist.

32. Encourage patient to express warmth appreciation, affection, and gratitude to others.

33. Assign patient to read "List of Aphorisms" in *Treating Type A Behaviors and Your Heart* (Friedman and Olmer) three times daily for 1 or 2 weeks; then to pick several to incorporate into his/her life.

34. Ask patient to list activities he/she could engage in for purely aesthetic enjoyment (e.g., visit an art museum, attend a symphony concert, hike in the woods, take painting lessons, etc.) and incorporate these into his/her life.

__. _____

_____

__. _____

_____

__. _____

_____

DIAGNOSTIC SUGGESTIONS

Axis I: 300.3   Obsessive-Compulsive Disorder
             300.02   Generalized Anxiety Disorder
             296.89   Bipolar II Disorder, Hypomanic
             _____   _____
             _____   _____

Axis II: 301.4   Obsessive-Compulsive Personality Disorder
             _____   _____
             _____   _____

VOCATIONAL STRESS

BEHAVIORAL DEFINITIONS

1. Feelings of anxiety and depression secondary to interpersonal conflict (perceived harassment, shunning, confrontation, etc.) with coworkers.
2. Feelings of inadequacy, fear, and failure secondary to severe business losses.
3. Fear of failure secondary to success or promotion that increases perceived expectations for greater success.
4. Rebellion against and/or conflicts with authority figures in the employment situation.
5. Feelings of anxiety and depression secondary to being fired or laid off, resulting in unemployment.
6. Anxiety related to perceived or actual job jeopardy.
7. Feelings of depression and anxiety related to complaints of job dissatisfaction or the stress of employment responsibilities.

—. _____
   _____
—. _____
   _____
—. _____
   _____

LONG-TERM GOALS

1. Improve satisfaction and comfort surrounding coworker relationships.
2. Increase sense of confidence and competence in dealing with work responsibilities.

244

3. Be cooperative with and accepting of supervision or direction in the work setting.
4. Increase sense of self-esteem and elevation of mood in spite of unemployment.
5. Increase job security as a result of more positive evaluation of performance by supervisor.
6. Engage in job-seeking behaviors consistently and with a reasonably positive attitude.
7. Increase job satisfaction and performance due to implementation of assertiveness and stress management strategies.

__. _____
_____
__. _____
_____
__. _____
_____

SHORT-TERM OBJECTIVES

1. Describe nature of conflicts with coworkers or supervisor. (1, 2)
2. Identify own role in the conflict with coworkers or supervisor. (1, 2, 11)
3. Identify any personal problems that may be causing conflict in the employment setting. (3, 4)
4. Replace projection of responsibility for conflict, feelings, or behavior with acceptance of responsibility for own behavior, feelings, and role in conflict. (4, 5, 6)
5. Identify behavioral changes that could be made in coworker or supervisor in-

THERAPEUTIC INTERVENTIONS

1. Clarify the nature of conflicts in work setting.
2. Help patient identify his/her own role in the conflict, attempting to represent the other party's point of view.
3. Explore possible role of substance abuse in vocational conflicts.
4. Explore the transfer of other personal problems to the employment situation.
5. Confront projection of responsibility for patient's behavior and feelings onto others.
6. Reinforce acceptance of responsibility for personal feelings and behavior.

teraction to help resolve conflict with coworkers or supervisors. (4, 5, 6, 7)

6. Rehearse interpersonal behaviors that will promote harmony with coworkers and supervisors. (1, 7, 8)

7. Implement assertiveness skills that allow for effective communication of needs and feelings without aggression or defensiveness. (9)

8. Develop and verbalize plan for constructive action to reduce vocational stress. (7, 10)

9. Identify patterns of similar conflict with people outside the work environment. (4, 11, 12)

10. Review family of origin history to determine roots for interpersonal conflict that are being reenacted in the work atmosphere. (12)

11. Review family of origin history to find roots of feelings of inadequacy, fear of failure, or fear of success. (13)

12. Verbalize feelings of fear, anger, and helplessness associated with the vocational stress. (14, 15)

13. Identify distorted cognitive messages associated with perception of job stress. (15, 16)

14. Develop more healthy, realistic cognitive messages that promote harmony with

7. Assign patient to write a plan for constructive action (e.g., polite compliance with directedness, initiate a smiling greeting, compliment other's work, avoid critical judgments, etc.) that contains various alternatives to coworker or supervisor conflict.

8. Use role-playing, behavioral rehearsal, and role reversal to increase the probability of positive encounters and reduce anxiety with others in employment situation or job search.

9. Train in assertiveness skills or refer to assertiveness-training class.

10. Process patient's proactive plan for addressing vocational issues.

11. Discuss possible patterns of interpersonal conflict that occur beyond the work setting.

12. Probe family of origin history for causes of current interpersonal conflict patterns.

13. Probe childhood history for roots of feelings of inadequacy, fear of failure, or fear of success.

14. Probe and clarify emotions surrounding the vocational stress.

15. Assess the distorted cognitive messages and schema connected with vocational stress.

others, self-acceptance, and self-confidence. (17, 18)

15. Verbalize an understanding of circumstances that led up to being terminated from employment. (1, 19)

16. Cease self-disparaging comments that are based on perceived failure at employment. (13, 17, 20, 21)

17. Discuss the effect that vocational stress has on feelings toward self and relationships with significant others. (21, 22)

18. Review success in all areas of life that affirm self as capable, likable, and of value. (20, 23, 24)

19. Outline plan for job search. (25, 26, 27)

20. Report on job search experiences and feelings surrounding these experiences. (28)

___. _____
_____
___. _____
_____
___. _____
_____

16. Confront catastrophizing the situation leading to immobilizing anxiety.

17. Train in the development of more realistic, healthy cognitive messages that relieve anxiety and depression.

18. Require patient to keep a daily record of self-defeating thoughts (thoughts of hopelessness, worthlessness, rejection, catastrophizing, negatively predicting the future, etc.), challenge each thought for accuracy, then replace each dysfunctional thought with one that is positive and self-enhancing.

19. Probe causes for termination of employment that may have been beyond patient's control.

20. Reinforce realistic self-appraisal of patient's successes and failures at employment.

21. Explore the effect of vocational stress on intra- and interpersonal dynamics with friends and family.

22. Facilitate a family therapy session in which feelings of family members can be aired and clarified regarding the vocational situation.

23. Assign patient to separately list his/her positive traits and talents, successful accomplishments, and then people who care for, respect, and value him/her. Process

these lists as a basis for genuine gratitude and self-worth.

24. Teach patient that the ultimate worth of an individual is not measured in material or vocational success but in service to a higher power and others.

25. Help patient develop a written job plan that contains specific obtainable objectives for job search.

26. Assign patient to choose jobs in want ads and ask friends or family about job opportunities.

27. Assign patient to attend a job search class or resume-writing seminar.

28. Monitor, encourage, and process patient's search for employment.

__. _____
    _____

__. _____
    _____

__. _____
    _____

DIAGNOSTIC SUGGESTIONS

Axis I:

309.0	Adjustment Disorder with Depressed Mood
300.4	Dysthymic Disorder
296.xx	Major Depressive Disorder
V62.2	Occupational Problem
309.24	Adjustment Disorder with Anxiety
303.90	Alcohol Dependence
304.20	Cocaine Dependence
304.80	Polysubstance Dependence
_____	_____

Axis II:

301.0	Paranoid Personality Disorder
301.81	Narcissistic Personality Disorder
301.7	Antisocial Personality Disorder
301.9	Personality Disorder NOS
_____	_____
_____	_____

Appendix A

BIBLIOTHERAPY SUGGESTIONS

Anger Management

Ellis, A. (1977). *Anger: How to Live With and Without It.* Secaucus, NJ: Citadel Press.

Lerner, H. (1985). *The Dance of Anger: A Woman's Guide to Changing the Patterns of Intimate Relationships.* New York: Harper Perennial.

McKay, M., Rogers, P., and McKay, J. (1989). *When Anger Hurts.* Oakland, CA: New Harbinger.

Rosellini, G., and Worden, M. (1986). *Of Course You're Angry.* San Francisco: Harper Hazelden.

Rubin, T. I. (1969). *The Angry Book.* New York: Macmillan.

Smedes, L. (1991). *Forgive and Forget: Healing the Hurts We Don't Deserve.* San Francisco: Harper.

Tavris, C. (1989). *Anger: The Misunderstood Emotion.* New York: Touchstone Books.

Weisinger, H. (1985). *Dr. Weisinger's Anger Work Out Book.* New York: Quill.

Antisocial Behavior

Carnes, Patrick (1983). *Out of the Shadows: Understanding Sexual Addictions.* Minneapolis, MN: CompCare.

Katherine, A. (1991). *Boundaries: Where You End and I Begin.* New York: Simon & Schuster.

Pittman, F. (1998). *Grow Up!* New York: Golden Books.

Williams, R., and Williams, V. (1993). *Anger Kills.* New York: Time Books.

Anxiety

Benson, H. (1975). *The Relaxation Response.* New York: William Morrow.
Burns, D. (1993). *Ten Days to Self-Esteem!* New York: William Morrow.
Davis, M., Eshelman, E., and McKay, M. (1988). *The Relaxation and Stress Reduction Workbook.* Oakland, CA: New Harbinger.
Hauck, P. (1975). *Overcoming Worry and Fear.* Philadelphia, PA: Westminster Press.
Jeffers, S. (1987). *Feel the Fear and Do It Anyway.* San Diego, CA: Harcourt Brace Jovanovich.
Marks, I. (1980). *Living with Fear: Understanding and Coping with Anxiety.* New York: McGraw-Hill.

Attention-Deficit Disorder (ADD)—Adult

Hallowell, E., and Ratey, J. (1994). *Driven to Distraction.* New York: Simon & Schuster.
Kelly, K., and Ramundo, P. (1994). *You Mean I'm Not Lazy, Stupid or Crazy.* Cincinnati, OH: Tyrell & Jerem Press.
Nadeau, K. (1996). *Adventures in Fast Forward.* New York: Brunner/Mazel.
Quinn, D., and Stern, J. (1991). *Putting on the Brakes.* New York: Magination Press.
Weis, Lynn. (1994). *The Attention Deficit Disorder In Adults Workbook.* Dallas, TX: Taylor Publishing.
Wender, P. (1987). *The Hyperactive Child, Adolescent and Adult.* New York: Oxford.

Borderline Personality

Cudney, M., and Handy, R. 1993. *Self-Defeating Behaviors.* San Francisco: HarperCollins.
Katherine, A. (1991). *Boundaries: Where You End and I Begin.* New York: Simon & Schuster.
Peurito, R. (1997). *Overcoming Anxiety.* New York: Henry Holt.

Chemical Dependence

Alcoholics Anonymous (1975). *Living Sober.* New York: A. A. World Service.
Alcoholics Anonymous (1976). *Alcoholics Anonymous: The Big Book.* New York: A. A. World Service.
Carnes, P. (1989). *A Gentle Path Through the Twelve Steps.* Minneapolis, MN: CompCare.
Drews, T. R. (1980). *Getting Them Sober: A Guide for Those Living with Alcoholism.* South Plainfield, NJ: Bridge Publishing.

Gorski, T., and Miller, M. (1986). *Staying Sober: A Guide to Relapse Prevention.* Independence, MO: Herald House Press.

Gorski, T. (1989–92). *The Staying Sober Workbook.* Independence, MO: Herald House Press.

Johnson, V. (1980). *I'll Quit Tomorrow.* New York: Harper & Row.

Kasl-Davis, C. (1992). *Many Roads, One Journey.* New York: HarperCollins.

Nuckals, C. (1989). *Cocaine: From Dependence to Recovery.* Blue Ridge Summit, PA: TAB Books.

Wilson, B. (1967). *As Bill Sees It.* New York: A. A. World Service.

Chemical Dependence—Relapse

Alcoholics Anonymous (1975). *Living Sober.* New York: A. A. World Service.

Alcoholics Anonymous (1976). *Alcoholics Anonymous: The Big Book.* New York: A. A. World Service.

Burns, D. (1993). *Ten Days to Self-Esteem!* New York: William Morrow.

Carnes, P. (1989). *A Gentle Path Through the Twelve Steps.* Minneapolis, MN: CompCare Publishing.

Doe, J. (1955). *The Golden Book of Resentments.* Indianapolis, IN: SMT Guild Inc.

Drews, T. R. (1980). *Getting Them Sober: A Guide for Those Living with Alcoholism.* South Plainfield, NJ: Bridge Publishing.

Gorski, T., and Miller, M. (1986). *Staying Sober: A Guide to Relapse Prevention.* Independence, MO: Herald House Press.

Gorski, T. (1989–92). *The Staying Sober Workbook.* Independence, MO: Herald House Press.

Johnson, V. (1980). *I'll Quit Tomorrow.* New York: Harper & Row.

Kasl-Davis, C. (1992). *Many Roads, One Journey.* New York: HarperCollins.

Larson, E. (1985). *Stage II Recovery: Life Beyond Addiction.* San Francisco, CA: Harper & Row.

Nuckals, C. (1989). *Cocaine: From Dependency to Recovery.* Blue Ridge Summit, PA: TAB Books.

Wilson, B. (1967). *As Bill Sees It.* New York: A. A. World Service.

Childhood Traumas

Black, C. (1980). *It Will Never Happen to Me.* Denver: MAC Publishing.

Bradshaw, J. (1990). *Homecoming.* New York: Bantam Books.

Gil, E. (1984). *Outgrowing the Pain: A Book for and About Adults Abused as Children.* New York: Dell Publishing.

Kushner, H. (1981). *When Bad Things Happen to Good People.* New York: Schocken Books.

Pittman, F. (1998). *Grow Up!* New York: Golden Books.

Powell, J. (1969). *Why I'm Afraid to Tell You Who I Am.* Allen, TX: Argus Communications.

Smedes, L. (1991). *Forgive and Forget: Healing the Hurts We Don't Deserve.* San Francisco: Harper.
Whitfield, C. (1987). *Healing the Child Within.* Deerfield Beach, FL: Health Communications, Inc.
Whitfield, C. (1990). *A Gift To Myself.* Deerfield Beach, FL: Health Communications, Inc.

Chronic Pain

Benson, H. (1975). *The Relaxation Response.* New York: William Morrow.
Benson, H. (1979). *The Mind / Body Effect.* New York: Simon & Schuster.
Burns, D. (1989). *The Feeling Good Handbook.* New York: Plume.
Burns, D. (1993). *Ten Days to Self Esteem!* New York: William Morrow.
Caudill, M. (1995). *Managing Pain before It Manages You.* New York: Guilford.
Duckro, P., Richardson, W., and Marshall, J. (1995). *Taking Control of Your Headaches.* New York: Guilford.
Fields, H. (1987). *Pain.* New York: McGraw Hill.
Hunter, M. (1996). *Making Peace with Chronic Pain.* New York: Brunner/ Mazel.
LeShan, L. (1984). *How to Meditate.* New York: Bantam Books.
Morris, D. (1991). *The Culture of Pain.* Berkely: University of California Press.
Siegel, B. (1989). *Peace, Love & Healing.* New York: Harper & Row.

Cognitive Deficits

Ellis, A., and Harper, R. (1974). *A New Guide to Rational Living.* Hollywood, CA: Wilshire Books.

Dependency

Alberti, R., and Emmons, M. (1990). *Your Perfect Right.* San Luis Obispo, CA: Impact.
Beattie, M. (1987). *Codependent No More: How to Stop Controlling Others & Start Caring for Yourself.* San Francisco: Harper.
Drews. T. R. (1980). *Getting Them Sober: A Guide for Those Living with Alcoholism.* South Plainfield, NJ: Bridge Publishing.
Evans, P. (1992). *The Verbally Abusive Relationship.* Holbrook, MA: Bob Adams, Inc.
Helmfelt, R., Minirth, F., and Meier, P. (1985). *Love Is a Choice.* Nashville, TN: Nelson.
Katherine, A. (1991). *Boundaries: Where You End and I Begin.* New York: Simon & Schuster.
Norwood, R. (1985). *Women Who Love Too Much.* Los Angeles: Tarcher.

Pittman, F. (1998). *Grow Up!* New York: Golden Books.

Smith, M. (1985). *When I Say No, I Feel Guilty.* New York: Bantam Books.

Walker, L. (1979). *The Battered Woman.* New York: Harper & Row.

Whitfield, C. (1990). *A Gift to Myself: A Personal Guide to Healing My Child Within.* Deerfield Beach, FL: Health Communications, Inc.

Whitfield, C. (1993). *Boundaries and Relationships: Knowing, Protecting and Enjoying the Self.* Deerfield Beach, FL: Health Communications, Inc.

Depression

Burns, D. (1980). *Feeling Good: The New Mood Therapy.* New York: Signet.

Burns, D. (1989). *The Feeling Good Handbook.* New York: Plume.

Butler, P. (1991). *Talking to Yourself: Learning the Language of Self-Affirmation.* New York: Stein and Day.

Dyer, W. (1974). *Your Erroneous Zones.* New York: Funk & Wagnalls.

Frankl, V. (1959). *Man's Search for Meaning.* New York: Simon & Schuster.

Geisel, T. (1990). *Oh, The Places You'll Go.* New York: Random House.

Hallinan, P. K. (1976). *One Day at a Time.* Minneapolis, MN: CompCare.

Hazelden Staff (1991). *Each Day a New Beginning.* Center City, MN: Hazelden.

Helmstetter, S. (1986). *What to Say When You Talk to Yourself.* New York: Fine Communications.

Knauth, P. (1977). *A Season in Hell.* New York: Pocket Books.

Leith, L. (1998). *Exercising Your Way to Better Mental Health.* Morgantown, WV: Fitness Information Technology.

Styron, W. (1990). *Darkness Visible.* New York: Random House.

Zonnebelt-Smeenge, S., and DeVries, R. (1998). *Getting to the Other Side of Grief: Overcoming the Loss of a Spouse.* Grand Rapids, MI: Baker.

Dissociation

Grateful Members of Emotional Health Anonymous (1982). *The Twelve Steps for Everyone . . . Who Really Wants Them.* Minneapolis, MN: CompCare.

Eating Disorder

Fairburn, C. (1995). *Overcoming Binge Eating.* New York: Guilford.

Hirschmann, J., and Munter, C. (1988). *Overcoming Overeating.* New York: Ballantine Books.

Hollis, J. (1985). *Fat Is a Family Affair.* New York: Harper & Row.

Rodin, J. (1993). *Body Traps.* New York: William Morrow.

Sacker, I., and Zimmer, M. (1987). *Dying to Be Thin.* New York: Warner Books.

Siegel, M., Brisman, J., and Weinshel, M. (1997). *Surviving an Eating Disorder.* San Francisco: HarperCollins.

Educational Deficits

de Boro, E. (1982). *de Boro's Thinking Course*. New York: Facts of Life Publishing.

Sandstrom, R. (1990). *The Ultimate Memory Book*. Granada, CA: Stepping Stones Books.

Family Conflict

Black, C. (1980). *It Will Never Happen to Me*. Denver: MAC Publishing.

Bloomfield, H., and Felder, L. (1983). *Making Peace with Your Parents*. New York: Random House.

Bradshaw, J. (1988). *On the Family*. Deerfield Beach, FL: Health Communications, Inc.

Cline, F., and Fay, J. (1990). *Parenting with Love and Logic*. Colorado Springs, CO: Pinon Press.

Faber, A., and Mazlish, E. (1987). *Siblings Without Rivalry*. New York: Norton.

Fassler, D., Lash, M., and Ivers, S. (1988). *Changing Families*. Burlington, VT: Waterfront Books.

Ginott, H. (1969). *Between Parent and Child*. New York: Macmillan.

Ginott, H. (1969). *Between Parent and Teenager*. New York: Macmillan.

Glenn, S., and Nelsen, J. (1989). *Raising Self-Reliant Children in a Self-Indulgent World*. Rocklin, CA: Prima.

Phelan, T. (1995). *1-2-3 Magic*. Glen Ellyn, IL: Child Management, Inc.

Steinberg, L., and Levine, A. (1990). *You and Your Adolescent: A Parents' Guide for Ages 10–20*. New York: Harper Perennial.

Female Sexual Dysfunction

Barbach, L. (1982). *For Each Other: Sharing Sexual Intimacy*. New York: Doubleday.

Comfort, A. (1991). *The New Joy of Sex*. New York: Crown.

Heiman, J., and LoPiccolo, J. (1988). *Becoming Orgasmic: A Sexual Growth Program for Women*. New York: Prentice-Hall.

Kaplan, H. S. (1975). *The Illustrated Manual of Sex Therapy*. New York: Quadrangle, New York Times Book Co.

McCarthy, B., and McCarthy, E. (1984). *Sexual Awareness*. New York: Carroll & Graf.

Penner, C., and Penner C. (1981). *The Gift of Sex*. Waco, TX: Word.

Valins, L. (1992). *When a Woman's Body Says No to Sex: Understanding and Overcoming Vaginismus*. New York: Penguin.

Zilbergeld, B. (1992). *The New Male Sexuality*. New York: Bantam.

Financial Stress

Abentrod, S. (1996). *10 Minute Guide to Beating Debt.* New York: Macmillan.
Burkett, L. (1989). *Debt Free Living.* Chicago: Moody Press.
Loungo, T. (1997). *10 Minute Guide to Household Budgeting.* New York: Macmillan.
Ramsey, D. (1997). *Financial Peace.* New York: Penguin Books.

Grief/Loss Unresolved

Colgrove, M., Bloomfield, H., and McWilliams, P. (1991). *How to Survive the Loss of a Love.* Los Angeles: Prelude Press.
Kushner, H. (1981). *When Bad Things Happen to Good People.* New York: Schocken Books.
Lewis, C. S. (1961). *A Grief Observed.* New York: Seabury Press.
Rando, T. (1991). *How to Go on Living When Someone You Love Dies.* New York: Bantam.
Schiff, N. (1977). *The Bereaved Parent.* New York: Crown.
Smedes, L. (1982). *How Can It Be All Right When Everything Is All Wrong.* San Francisco: Harper.
Smedes, L. (1991). *Forgive and Forget: Healing the Hurts We Don't Deserve.* San Francisco: Harper.
Westberg, G. (1962). *Good Grief.* Philadelphia: Augsburg Fortress Press.
Wolterstorff, N. (1987). *Lament for a Son.* Grand Rapids, MI: Eerdmans.
Zonnebelt-Smeenge, S., and DeVries, R. (1998). *Getting to the Other Side of Grief: Overcoming the Loss of a Spouse.* Grand Rapids, MI: Baker.

Impulse Control Disorder

Helmstetter, S. (1986). *What to Say When You Talk to Yourself.* New York: Fine Communications.
Kelly, K., and Ramundo, P. (1994). *You Mean I'm Not Lazy, Stupid or Crazy: A Self-Help Book for Adults with Attention Deficit Disorder.* Cincinnati, OH: Tyrell & Jerem Press.
Wender, P. (1987). *The Hyperactive Child, Adolescent and Adult.* New York: Oxford.

Intimate Relationship Conflicts

Abrahms-Spring, J. (1996). *After the Affair.* New York: Harper Collins.
Bach, G., and Wyden, P. (1976). *The Intimate Enemy: How to Fight Fair in Love and Marriage.* New York: Avon Books.

Colgrove, M., Bloomfield, H., and McWilliams, P. (1991). *How to Survive the Loss of a Love.* Los Angeles: Prelude Press.

Fisher, B. (1981). *ReBuilding: When Your Relationship Ends.* San Luis Obispo, CA: Impact.

Fromm, E. (1956). *The Art of Loving.* New York: Harper & Row.

Gorski, T. (1993). *Getting Love Right: Learning the Choices of Healthy Intimacy.* New York: Simon & Schuster.

Gray, J. (1993). *Men and Women and Relationships: Making Peace with the Opposite Sex.* Hillsboro, OR: Beyond Words.

Gray, J. (1992). *Men Are From Mars, Women Are From Venus.* New York: HarperCollins.

Harley, W. (1994). *His Needs, Her Needs: Building an Affair-Proof Marriage.* Grand Rapids, MI: Revell.

Hendrix, H. (1988). *Getting the Love You Want.* New York: Henry Holt.

Lerner, H. (1989). *The Dance of Intimacy: A Woman's Guide to Courageous Acts of Change in Key Relationships.* New York: Harper Perennial.

Lindbergh, A. (1955). *A Gift from the Sea.* New York: Pantheon.

Markman, H., Stanley S., and Blumberg, S. (1994). *Fighting for Your Marriage.* San Francisco: Jossey-Bass.

Schnarch, D. (1997). *Passionate Marriage.* New York: Norton.

Legal Conflicts

Carnes, P. (1983). *Out of the Shadows: Understanding Sexual Addictions.* Minneapolis, MN: CompCare.

Williams, R., and Williams, V. (1993). *Anger Kills.* New York: Time Books.

Low Self-Esteem

Branden, N. (1994). *The Six Pillars of Self-Esteem.* New York: Bantam Books.

Burns, D. (1993). *Ten Days to Self Esteem!* New York: William Morrow.

Helmstetter, S. (1986). *What to Say When You Talk to Yourself.* New York: Fine Communications.

McKay, M., and Fanning, P. (1987). *Self-Esteem.* Oakland, CA: New Harbinger.

Shapiro, L. (1993). *Building Blocks of Self Esteem.* King of Prussia, PA: Center for Applied Psychology.

Zimbardo, P. (1987). *Shyness: What It Is and What to Do About It.* Reading, MA: Addison-Wesley.

Male Sexual Dysfunction

Comfort, A. (1991). *The New Joy of Sex.* New York: Crown.

Kaplan, H. S. (1975). *The Illustrated Manual of Sex Therapy.* New York: Quadrangle, New York Times Book Co.

McCarthy, B., and McCarthy, E. (1984). *Sexual Awareness*. New York: Carroll & Graf.

Penner, C., and Penner, C. (1981). *The Gift of Sex*. Waco, TX: Word.

Zilbergeld, B. (1992). *The New Male Sexuality*. New York: Bantam.

Mania or Hypomania

Grateful Members of Emotional Health Anonymous (1987). *The Twelve Steps for Everyone . . . Who Really Wants Them*. Minneapolis, MN: CompCare.

Medical Issues

Friedman, M., and Ulmer, P. (1984). *Treating Type A Behavior and Your Heart*. New York: Alfred Knopf.

Obsessive-Compulsive Disorder (OCD)

Burns, D. (1993). *Ten Days to Self-Esteem!* New York: William Morrow.

Foa, E., and Wilson, R. (1991). *S.T.O.P. Obsessing: How to Overcome Your Obsessions and Compulsions*. New York: Bantam Books.

Levenkron, S. (1991). *Obsessive-Compulsive Disorders*. New York: Warner Books.

Paranoid Ideation

Burns, D. (1989). *The Feeling Good Handbook*. New York: Plume.

Cudney, M., and Hard, R. (1991). *Self-Defeating Behaviors*. San Francisco: HarperCollins.

Ross, J. (1994). *Triumph over Fear*. New York: Bantam Books.

Phobia-Panic/Agoraphobia

Gold, M. (1988). *The Good News About Panic, Anxiety, and Phobias*. New York: Villard/Random House.

Marks, I. (1980). *Living with Fear: Understanding and Coping with Anxiety*. New York: McGraw-Hill.

Swede, S., and Jaffe, S. (1987). *The Panic Attack Recovery Book*. New York: New American Library.

Wilson, R. (1986). *Don't Panic: Taking Control of Anxiety Attacks*. New York: Harper & Row.

Posttraumatic Stress Disorder (PTSD)

Frankel, V. (1959). *Man's Search for Meaning.* Boston: Beacon Press.
Jeffers, S. (1987). *Feel the Fear and Do It Anyway.* New York: Random House.
Leith, L. (1998). *Exercising Your Way to Better Mental Health.* Morgantown, WV: Fitness Information Technology.
Matsakis, A. (1992). *I Can't Get Over It: A Handbook for Trauma Survivors.* Oakland, CA: New Harbinger.
Simon, S., and Simon, S. (1990). *Forgiving: How to Make Peace with Your Past and Get On with Your Life.* New York: Warner Books.

Psychoticism

Torrey, M. D., and Fuller, E. (1988). *Surviving Schizophrenia: A Family Manual.* New York: Harper & Row.

Sexual Abuse

Bass, E., and Davis, L. (1988). *The Courage to Heal: A Guide for Women Survivors of Child Sexual Abuse.* San Francisco: HarperCollins.
Bradshaw, J. (1988). *Healing the Shame That Binds You.* Deerfield Beach, FL: Health Communications, Inc.
Burns, D. (1993). *Ten Days to Self Esteem!* New York: William Morrow.
Davis, L. (1990). *The Courage to Heal Workbook: For Men & Women Survivors of Child Sexual Abuse.* San Francisco: HarperCollins.
Forward, S., and Buck, C. (1978). *Betrayal of Innocence: Incest and Its Devastation.* New York: Penguin Books.
Fossum, M. A., and Mason, M. J. (1986). *Facing Shame: Families in Recovery.* New York: Norton.
Gil, E. (1984). *Outgrowing the Pain: A Book for and About Adults Abused as Children.* New York: Dell Publishing.
Kaufman, G. (1992). *Shame: The Power of Caring.* Rochester, VT: Schenkman Books.
Simon, S., and Simon, S. (1990). *Forgiving: How to Make Peace with Your Past and Get On with Your Life.* New York: Warner Books.
Smedes, L. (1991). *Forgive and Forget: Healing the Hurts We Don't Deserve.* San Francisco: Harper.

Sleep Disturbance

Dotto, L. (1990). *Losing Sleep: How Your Sleeping Habits Affect Your Life.* New York: William Morrow.
Hewish, J. (1985). *Relaxation.* Chicago: NTC Publishing Group.

Leith, L. (1998). *Exercising Your Way to Better Mental Health.* Morgantown, WV: Fitness Information Technology.

Social Discomfort

Bradshaw, J. (1988). *Healing the Shame That Binds You.* Deerfield Beach, FL: Health Communications, Inc.

Burns, D. (1985). *Intimate Connections: The New Clinically Tested Program for Overcoming Loneliness.* New York: William Morrow.

Burns, D. (1993). *Ten Days to Self Esteem!* New York: William Morrow.

Dyer, W. (1978). *Pulling Your Own Strings.* New York: T. Crowell.

Fossum, M. A., and Mason, M. J. (1986). *Facing Shame: Families in Recovery.* New York: Norton.

Harris, A., and Harris, T. (1969). *I'm OK You're OK.* New York: Harper & Row.

James, M., and Jongeward, D. (1971). *Born to Win.* Reading, MA: Addison-Wesley.

Nouwen, H. (1975). *Reaching Out.* New York: Doubleday.

Zimbardo, P. (1987). *Shyness: What It Is and What to Do About It.* Reading, MA: Addison-Wesley.

Somatization

Benson, H. (1980). *The Mind-Body Effect.* New York: Simon & Schuster.

Grateful Members of Emotional Health Anonymous (1987). *The Twelve Steps for Everyone . . . Who Really Wants Them.* Minneapolis, MN: CompCare.

Spiritual Confusion

Armstrong, K. (1993). *A History of God.* New York: Alfred Knopf.

Augustine, St. (1949). *The Confessions of St. Augustine.* New York: Random House.

Cleaver, E. (1992). *The Soul on Fire.* Grand Rapids, MI: Zondervan.

Foster, Richard. (1978). *Celebration of Discipline.* New York: Harper & Row.

Helmfelt, R., and Fowler, R. (1990). *Serenity: A Companion for 12 Step Recovery.* Nashville, TN: Nelson.

Keen, S. (1994). *Hymns to an Unknown God.* New York: Bantam Books.

Lewis, C. S. (1955). *Surprised by Joy.* New York: Harcourt Brace.

Merton, T. (1948). *The Seven Storey Mountain.* New York: Harcourt Brace.

Miles, J. (1995). *God: A Biography.* New York: Alfred Knopf.

Moore, T. (1992). *Care of the Soul.* New York: HarperCollins.

Norris, K. (1996). *The Cloister Walk.* New York: Riverhead Books.

Peck, M. S. (1978). *The Road Less Traveled.* New York: Simon & Schuster.

Peck, M. S. (1993). *Further Along the Road Less Traveled.* New York: Simon & Schuster.

Presnall, L. (1959). *Search for Serenity: And How to Achieve It*. Salt Lake City, UT: V.A.F. Publishing.

Suicidal Ideation

Butler, P. (1991). *Talking to Yourself: Learning the Language of Self-Affirmation*. New York: Stein and Day.
Hutschnecker, A. (1951). *The Will to Live*. New York: Cornerstone Library.
Seligman, M. (1990). *Learned Optimism: The Skill to Conquer Life's Obstacles, Large and Small*. New York: Pocket Books.

Type A Behavior

Friedman, M., and Olmer, D. (1984). *Treating Type A Behaviors and Your Heart*. New York: Alfred Knopf.
Glasser, W. (1976). *Positive Addiction*. San Francisco: HarperCollins.
Peck, M. S. (1978). *The Road Less Traveled*. New York: Simon & Schuster.
Peck, M. S. (1993). *Further Along the Road Less Traveled*. New York: Simon & Schuster.
Pirsig, R. (1974). *Zen and the Art of Motorcycle Maintenance*. New York: William Morrow.
Robinson, B. (1993). *Overdoing It*. Deerfield Beach, FL: Health Communications, Inc.

Vocational Stress

Bolles, R. (1992). *What Color Is Your Parachute?* Berkeley, CA: Ten-Speed Press.
Charland, R. (1993). *Career Shifting: Starting Over in a Changing Economy*. Holbrook, MA: Bob Adams.
Jandt, F. (1985). *Win-Win Negotiating: Turning Conflict into Agreement*. New York: John Wiley & Sons.
Weiss, R. (1990). *Staying the Course: The Emotional and Social Lives of Men Who Do Well at Work*. New York: Free Press.

Appendix B

INDEX OF *DSM-IV* CODES ASSOCIATED WITH PRESENTING PROBLEMS

Academic Problem   **V62.3**
Educational Deficits

Acute Stress Disorder   **308.3**
Posttraumatic Stress Disorder

Adjustment Disorder   **309.xx**
Posttraumatic Stress Disorder

**Adjustment Disorder
with Anxiety**   **309.24**
Anxiety
Intimate Relationship Conflicts
Vocational Stress

**Adjustment Disorder
with Depressed Mood**   **309.0**
Depression
Grief/Loss Unresolved
Intimate Relationship Conflicts
Vocational Stress

**Adjustment Disorder with
Disturbance of Conduct**   **309.3**
Antisocial Behavior
Grief/Loss Unresolved
Legal Conflicts

Adult Antisocial Behavior   **V71.01**
Chemical Dependence
Legal Conflicts

**Agoraphobia without History
of Panic Disorder**   **300.22**
Phobia-Panic/Agoraphobia

Alcohol Abuse   **305.00**
Attention Deficit Disorder—Adult
Chemical Dependence
Chemical Dependence—Relapse
Posttraumatic Stress Disorder

Alcohol Dependence   **303.90**
Attention Deficit Disorder—Adult
Antisocial Behavior
Chemical Dependence
Chemical Dependence—Relapse
Cognitive Deficits
Dissociation
Family Conflicts
Legal Conflicts
Medical Issues
Obsessive-Compulsive Behaviors
Posttraumatic Stress Disorder
Sexual Abuse
Vocational Stress

**Alcohol-Induced Persisting
Amnestic Disorder**   **291.1**
Chemical Dependence
Chemical Dependence—Relapse
Cognitive Deficits

**Alcohol-Induced Persisting
Dementia**   291.2
Chemical Dependence
Chemical Dependence—Relapse
Cognitive Deficits

**Amnestic Disorder Due to
(Axis III Disorder)**   294.0
Cognitive Deficits

Amnestic Disorder NOS   294.8
Cognitive Deficits

Anorexia Nervosa   307.1
Eating Disorder

**Antisocial Personality
Disorder**   301.7
Anger Management
Antisocial Behavior
Chemical Dependence
Chemical Dependence—Relapse
Childhood Traumas
Family Conflicts
Financial Stress
Impulse Control Disorder
Legal Conflicts
Vocational Stress

**Attention-Deficit/Hyperactivity
Disorder, Predominately
Inattentive Type**   314.00
Attention Deficit Disorder—Adult

**Attention-Deficit/Hyperactivity
Disorder, Predominately
Hypersensitive-Impulsive
Type**   314.01
Attention Deficit Disorder—Adult

**Attention-Deficit/
Hyperactivity Disorder NOS**   314.9
Attention Deficit Disorder—Adult

Anxiety Disorder NOS   300.00
Anxiety
Family Conflicts
Intimate Relationship Conflicts
Obsessive-Compulsive Behaviors
Spiritual Confusion

**Avoidant Personality
Disorder**   301.82
Dependency
Obsessive-Compulsive Behaviors
Sexual Abuse
Social Discomfort

Bereavement   V62.82
Depression
Grief/Loss Unresolved

Bipolar Disorder NOS   296.80
Mania or Hypomania

Bipolar I Disorder, Manic   296.4x
Financial Stress

Bipolar I Disorder   296.xx
Attention Deficit Disorder—Adult
Anger Management
Depression
Low Self-Esteem
Mania or Hypomania
Psychoticism
Suicidal Ideation

Bipolar II Disorder   296.89
Anger Management
Depression
Financial Stress
Low Self-Esteem
Mania or Hypomania
Psychoticism
Suicidal Ideation

Body Dysmorphic Disorder   300.7
Somatization

**Borderline Intellectual
Functioning**   V62.89
Educational Deficits

**Borderline Personality
Disorder**   301.83
Anger Management
Borderline Personality
Dependency
Family Conflicts
Impulse Control Disorder
Posttraumatic Stress Disorder
Suicidal Ideation

Dysthymic Disorder   300.4
  Borderline Personality
  Chemical Dependence
  Chemical Dependence—Relapse
  Childhood Traumas
  Dependency
  Depression
  Family Conflicts
  Grief/Loss Unresolved
  Intimate Relationship Conflicts
  Low Self-Esteem
  Sexual Abuse
  Sleep Disturbance
  Social Discomfort
  Somatization
  Spiritual Confusion
  Suicidal Ideation
  Vocational Stress

Eating Disorder NOS   307.50
  Eating Disorder

**Female Dyspareunia Due to
(Axis III Disorder)**   625.0
  Female Sexual Dysfunction

**Female Hypoactive Sexual
Desire Disorder Due to
(Axis III Disorder)**   625.8
  Female Sexual Dysfunction

Female Orgasmic Disorder   302.73
  Female Sexual Dysfunction

**Female Sexual Arousal
Disorder**   302.72
  Female Sexual Dysfunction

**Generalized Anxiety
Disorder**   300.02
  Anxiety
  Childhood Trauma
  Sexual Abuse
  Type A Behavior

**Hypoactive Sexual Desire
Disorder**   302.71
  Female Sexual Dysfunction
  Male Sexual Dysfunction

Hypochondriasis   300.7
  Medical Issues
  Somatization

**Impulse Control
Disorder NOS**   312.30
  Attention Deficit Disorder—Adult
  Impulse Control Disorder

**Intermittent Explosive
Disorder**   312.34
  Anger Management
  Antisocial Behavior
  Chemical Dependence
  Family Conflicts
  Impulse Control Disorder
  Intimate Relationship Conflicts

Kleptomania   312.32
  Impulse Control Disorder
  Legal Conflicts

Major Depressive Disorder   296.xx
  Childhood Trauma
  Depression
  Financial Stress
  Low Self-Esteem
  Obsessive-Compulsive Behaviors
  Posttraumatic Stress Disorder
  Psychoticism
  Sexual Abuse
  Sleep Disturbance
  Social Discomfort
  Spiritual Confusion
  Vocational Stress

**Major Depressive Disorder,
Recurrent**   296.3
  Borderline Personality
  Chronic Pain
  Depression
  Grief/Loss Unresolved
  Suicidal Ideation

**Major Depressive Disorder,
Single Episode**   296.2x
  Depression
  Grief/Loss Unresolved
  Suicidal Ideation

**Maladaptive Health Behaviors
Affecting (Axis III Disorder)** 316
  Medical Issues

**Male Dyspareunia Due to
(Axis III Disorder)**   608.89
  Male Sexual Dysfunction

TheraBiller with TheraScheduler™

The Computerized Mental Health Office Manager

Spend More Time on Patients - Not Paperwork

TheraBiller w/TheraScheduler™ is our new Windows®-based software package designed specifically to help you manage your mental health practice....

Powerful...
- TheraBiller™ with TheraScheduler™ integrates seamlessly with TheraScribe® 3.0: The Computerized Assistant to Psychotherapy Treatment Planning. Although each program can be used independently, by using them in cooperatively you'll get a complete office management system, with automatic common data sharing and one-button toggling
- Completes pre-printed or program-generated HCFA forms, and produces easy-to-read, professional-looking invoices and aged accounts receivable reports
- Tracks managed care information (sessions authorized, sessions used, capitated fees, hourly fees, etc.)
- Built-in electronic billing compatibility (claims module interfaces with **InStream Provider Network™**)
- Electronic cardex which prints mailing labels and tracks contact information

Flexible...
- Robust reporting options — print or preview billing summaries and usage statistics by provider, patient, or time-frame
- Full quick-reference DSM-IV and CPT code libraries (including new G-codes)
- Data export to Quicken® and MicroSoft Money®, as well as common spreadsheet and accounting programs (e.g., Excel®, Peachtree®, etc.)
- Perfect for solo providers or large group practices (the stand-alone version handles an unlimited number of providers, and a network version is also available)

User-Friendly...
- Features the same intuitive interface as Wiley's best-selling TheraScribe ®3.0.
- Includes a handy Billing Wizard to guide you through the billing process and a Report Wizard that helps you select report parameters
- Built-in appointment book, with daily, weekly, monthly scheduling for an unlimited number of providers— updates automatically when you book a session in TheraScribe® 3.0
- Password-protected to safeguard confidential data. Varying levels of data access may be assigned to each user

---

System Requirements
IBM®-compatible 486DX * 8 MB RAM (12MB recommended) * 10MB Hard Disk Space
VGA display (SVGA recommended) * Windows® 3.1

For more information on *TheraBiller™*, fill in this coupon, and mail it to: M. Fellin, John Wiley & Sons, Inc., 605 Third Avenue, New York, NY 10158.

Name _____

Affiliation _____

Address _____

City/State/Zip _____

Phone _____

Visit our web site and download a free demo: www.wiley.com/therabiller

 WILEY
Publishers Since 1807

TheraScribe® 3.0 for Windows®

The Computerized Assistant to Psychotherapy Treatment Planning

→ Used in thousands of behavioral health practices and treatment facilities, *TheraScribe® 3.0* is a state-of-the-art Windows®-based treatment planning program which rapidly generates comprehensive treatment plans meeting the requirements of all major accrediting agencies and most third-party payers.

→ In just minutes, this user-friendly program enables you to create customized treatment plans by choosing from thousands of prewritten built-in short-term goals, long-term objectives, therapeutic interventions, automated progress notes, and much more.

→ This networkable software also tracks treatment outcome, stores clinical pathways, and provides ample room for narrative patient histories, treatment summaries, and discharge notes.

→ And best of all, this flexible system can be expanded to include the data in this *Complete Adult Treatment Planner, 2nd Edition.*

✎COMPLETE ADULT 2E Upgrade to THERASCRIBE® 3.0✎

The behavioral definitions, goals, objectives, and interventions from this *Complete Adult Treatment Planner 2E* can be imported into *TheraScribe® 3.0: The Computerized Assistant to Treatment Planning*. For purchase and pricing information, please send in the coupon below.

- -

For more information about *TheraScribe® 3.0* or the *Complete Adult 2E Upgrade,* fill in this coupon, and mail it to: M. Fellin, John Wiley & Sons, Inc., 605 Third Avenue, New York, NY 10158

❑ Please send me information on TheraScribe® 3.0
❑ Please send me information on the Complete Adult 2E Upgrade to TheraScribe® 3.0

Name _____

Affiliation _____

Address _____

City/State/Zip _____

Phone _____

WILEY
Publishers Since 1807

ABOUT THE DISK

TheraScribe® 3.0 Library Module Installation

The enclosed disk contains files to upgrade your TheraScribe® 3.0 program to include the behavioral definitions, goals, objectives, and interventions from *The Complete Adult Psychotherapy Treatment Planner, Second Edition.*

Note: You must have TheraScribe® 3.0 for Windows installed on your computer in order to use *The Complete Adult Psychotherapy Treatment Planner, Second Edition* library module.

To install the library module, please follow these steps:

1. Place the library module disk in your floppy drive.
2. Log in to TheraScribe® 3.0 as the Administrator using the name "Admin" and your administrator password.
3. On the Main Menu, press the "GoTo" button and choose the Options menu item.
4. Press the "Import Library" button.
5. On the Import Library Module screen, choose your floppy disk drive a:\ from the list and press "Go". Note: It may take a few minutes to import the data from the floppy disk to your computer's hard disk.
6. When the installation is complete the library module data will be available in your TheraScribe® 3.0 program.

Note: If you have a network version of TheraScribe® 3.0 installed, you should import the library module one time only. After importing the data, the library module data will be available to all network users.

User Assistance

If you need assistance using this TheraScribe® 3.0 add-on module, contact Wiley Technical Support at:

Phone: 212-850-6753
Fax: 212-850-6800 (Attention: Wiley Technical Support)
E-mail: techhelp@wiley.com

---

*Note: This section applies only to the book with disk edition, ISBN 0-471-31957-0.

For information on how to install disk, refer to the **About the Disk** section on page 277.

WILEY
Publishers Since 1807
